living in dependency
and wonder

Journals in the Being with God series

Hiddenness and Manifestation
The Nature of God
Crafted Prayer
Beholding and Becoming
The Language of Promise
Towards a Powerful Inner Life
God's Keeping Power
Living in Dependency and Wonder

an
interactive
journal

book seven

being with God series

living in dependency
and wonder

Graham Cooke

Brilliant Book House

Brilliant Book House
6391 Leisure Town Road
Vacaville, California 95687
USA
www.brilliantbookhouse.com

Requests for information regarding Graham's ministry should be
addressed to:
Graham Cooke
Future Training Institute
6391 Leisure Town Road
Vacaville, California
USA
office@grahamcooke.com
www.grahamcooke.com

ISBN

declaration

To walk with God in the high places we must lose our fear. Fear can only be lost in the desert, in the crucible of warfare, inferiority and internal struggle. In the place where only God can shelter you. Only His Comfort works. All is stripped bare and we come to rest in His goodness.

The passion of God that kills our strength now nurtures our weakness into a place of joyful vulnerability. Through the lens of our own inadequacy we begin to get glimpses of His sovereignty and all supremacy. Our hearts and minds are washed in His goodness. Revelation lifts us to the realm of a different reality and peace sets in.

Every obstacle and opposition is an opportunity to rest in the love of the Father. We enter every problem through grace in which we stand. Our wonder grows as we learn the joy of dependency.

I dedicate this book to the following people. Some have taught me personally, others I have observed from

near and afar ... many I count as friends and fellow
children in the kingdom.

Uncle Sid and Harry Greenwood from Chard, England
who pioneered living by faith as a reality to me, not just
a concept. Bob and Jean Acheson who exampled it daily
with great joy and simplicity. Arthur Burt who opened
up a dimension of the Spirit so profound it shattered my
mediocrity; much pain came from it, but I am glad and
grateful. Dee and Maggie, two wonderful elderly ladies
who lived by the Spirit and always gave me hope.

Ruth Fazal, composer and concert violinist, and a
lover of God and simplicity. Randy Clark, who I once
spent 10 days with in a bunker and who gave me more
than I gave him; time is still on my side Randy ... I'll get
you back!

John and Carol Arnott whose sheer delight in the
Father is intoxicating. Bill Johnson, who makes me want
to fold myself in his suitcase so I can travel with him. I
think America is going to have to find a new definition
for the word "awesome".

Richard Holcomb who makes me laugh when we're
fishing and cry when we're worshiping. Finally to Mike
Bickle, a friend who by his passion for Jesus never fails
to call up a greater love in my own heart when I am
around him.

introduction

My journey of learning the wonder of dependency
exploded into a different dimension five years ago with
a simple dream. In the dream, I was taken back to a time
of great rebellion and disobedience in my life, a time
when I wasn't "walking with the Lord," as Christians say.
I found myself reliving an awful situation from more
than twenty years ago.

As the story of my sin unfolded before my eyes, the
most incredible thing happened. It was as if God called a
time-out: everything just froze. The whole scene stood
still, as if it were in suspended animation.

Suddenly, Jesus stepped into the picture and looked at
me. I was shocked – and a bit ashamed – to see Him there
in the midst of my sin. But Jesus had a message for me.

"Grae," He said gently, "it wasn't your disobedience
or your rebellion that grieved Me. Son, I dealt with those
issues on the Cross. What grieved Me is that you never
saw what I wanted to be for you. You never understood
what I wanted to give you."

Jesus, the Master of everything – including dramatic timing – paused for a few seconds before continuing.

"If you had known what I wanted to be for you, this is how the situation would have turned out," He said, turning my attention back to the scene. The whole dream played out as if I had responded perfectly to God. In that instant, I saw what could have been. I woke up, feeling clean and new inside, and suddenly very aware of the depths of God's love for me.

Since that dream, I have begun to understand the power of our current circumstances to release more of God into our lives. Nothing out there in the world can affect me negatively when I ask God for His perspective and more of His character. It is possible to go into every situation intrigued, excited, and expectant for what God wants to show us.

Earlier in my ministry, God had put me on a journey into the *heights* of His love. He showed me things about His splendor and glory that I could never have imagined. But now, I am on a journey to discover the *depths* of His love. This is the true joy of dependency: that we can give thanks to God in every circumstance of our lives. I have meticulously gone through my past – even with its horrible rebellion, sin and abuse – and given thanks to God for every stage of it. I have forgiven anyone who has ever hurt me. I can't think of a single situation I haven't given thanks for.

Everything that God is doing in our lives is

intentionally relational. To walk with Him, therefore, we must also be intentionally relational – with Him and with others. God, in His wisdom, allows what He could easily prevent by His power. In everything, He is constant and in charge: sometimes He leads us into situations that are brilliant, and other times, He leads us into things that are difficult. But God's commitment to us never wavers. Every situation in life is about God wanting to give Himself to us.

Right now, our lives could be good, bad, or ugly, but we can be joyful knowing that God has designed our current circumstances to enable us to see a part of Him that we couldn't see at any other time.

The question we should never ask of God is, "Why?" The why question will never be answered on earth, because it's the wrong question. The question we must ask is, "What is this for?" We must see what Jesus wants to be for us in every situation. God always wants to be true to His name, to be the "I AM." Whatever is happening in your life right now, I AM is with you.

Together with Jesus, we can walk in the high places of the Spirit, and the low places of the soul, but only if we come to the simple understanding of who I AM truly is.

Galatians 5:22–23 is a Bible passage we have all read many times: it is a staple of Sunday School curriculum and charismatic preachers everywhere. *"But the fruit of the Spirit is love, joy, peace, longsuffering, kindness, goodness, faithfulness, gentleness, self-control,"* the

Apostle Paul wrote. The words should prick our consciences but many of us have forgotten what the fruit of the Spirit really means after years of sermons, Christian merchandising, and other uses.

Fortunately for us, God lives by the fruit of the Spirit. Every fiber of His being exudes these fruit. If God didn't exercise self-control, we'd all be dead. If it weren't for His kindness, we'd all be lost. If it weren't for His joy, we'd be heartbroken.

God's life is marked by another quality: generosity. All things have been given freely to us, the Bible says. Whatever we need in life is given to us by the hand of God. When we have a need, God's answer is always "Me." Everything is yes and amen in Christ. We must catch the extravagant generosity of God and allow His fruit of the Spirit to pervade our lives.

Jesus was passionate about giving us the fruit of the Spirit. *"A new commandment I give to you, that you love one another; as I have loved you, that you also love one another,"* He said in John 13:34. *"These things I have spoken to you, that My joy may remain in you, and that your joy may be full,"* He added in John 15:11. *"Peace I leave with you, My peace I give to you,"* Jesus said in John 14:27.

An amazing relationship exists between God's total capability and our corresponding weakness. Serving Him isn't just about recognizing how small we are, but about understanding how huge He is. We live in the tension of it all: He's big, we're small; He's strong, we're weak – let's all laugh about it together. The only thing we can do is marvel at how incredible He is. Every situation in life is a journey where God teaches us more about Himself. I don't think a day goes by where God doesn't show us more about who He is.

I believe that we are in a season when God wants to *"turn the hearts of the fathers to the children, and the hearts of the children to their fathers,"* as Malachi prophesied. Because of that, being a good father is high on God's agenda. He longs to father us into deeper places in the Spirit. We can partner with God in this process of fatherhood: after all, we must become child-like in order for Him to be our Dad. It's vital for us to be child-like – it's the only way we can grow in Christian maturity.

Being child-like isn't a matter of regressing into a lower place in the natural. It's actually about advancing into a greater place of life in the Spirit. Our innocence and purity must be recovered for us to live as children in the Father's house. The Kingdom of God belongs to those who can develop and maintain a child-like sense of wonder about God's majesty.

Graham Cooke
March 2004

living in dependency and wonder

love your neighbor

The gathered crowd was buzzing with a mix of excitement and skepticism. The enthusiastic ones were still talking about the incredible number of healings they had just seen performed. So many people had been healed that the crowd was clamoring just to touch the Nazarene carpenter who had made it all happen. What would He do next? Could He be the long-awaited Messiah, sent by God to deliver His chosen people from the iron grip of the Romans? There hadn't been this level of excitement in Israel since John the Baptist's first sermons by the river Jordan.

The skeptics were a little calmer in their assessment. The healings were nice, but perhaps the crowd had just given into emotionalism. After all, they had seen a lot of so-called messiahs come and go, and nothing had ever changed. The Romans still ruled. What did this Man have that those other failed deliverers didn't? Did Israel need another John the Baptist, stirring up outrageous hopes of freedom and victory that were sure to be dashed?

In the midst of it all, Jesus Christ climbed a small hill and began to speak. This Sermon on the Mount, as history would call it, was a world-changing moment. Luke 6:27 – 36 chronicles Jesus' words:

> *But I say to you who hear: Love your enemies, do good to those who hate you, bless those who curse you, and pray for those who spitefully use you. To him who strikes you on the one cheek, offer the other also. And from him who takes away your cloak, do not withhold your tunic either. Give to everyone who asks of you. And from him who takes away your goods do not ask them back. And just as you want men to do to you, you also do to them likewise.*
>
> *But if you love those who love you, what credit is that to you? For even sinners love those who love them. And if you do good to those who do good to you, what credit is that to you? For even sinners do the same. And if you lend to those from whom you hope to receive back, what credit is that to you? For even sinners lend to sinners to receive as much back. But love your enemies, do good, and lend, hoping for nothing in return; and your reward will be great, and you will be sons of the Most High. For He is kind to the unthankful and evil. Therefore be merciful, just as your Father also is merciful.*

Jesus' message that day, 2,000 years ago, can be boiled down into a simple phrase: "Love those who are incapable of loving you." It was an odd thing for a deliverer to preach. Be the first to love, the first to bless, the first to give. Give to anyone who asks. Give as a way of life.

Jesus wasn't concerned with earthly empires or people's perspectives of what a Messiah should look like. He was on a mission to deliver a statement about the nature of God and the nature of His Kingdom.

Nothing has changed since that Sermon on the Mount. Jesus still deliberately and mischievously takes all of our fears of being used, abused, and taken for granted, and makes us a promise: *"Love your enemies, do good, and lend, hoping for nothing in return; and your reward will be great, and you will be sons of the Most High."* When we depend on God – and no one else – to validate and reward us, our joy will be complete.

> "Blessed are the merciful, for they shall obtain mercy."
> Jesus Christ

innocence in the kingdom

"Blessed are the pure in heart, for they shall see God," Jesus said in His Sermon. What an intriguing comment! From it, we can safely say that a lack of innocence detracts from our ability to see God. Innocence. Purity. Child-likeness. Wonder. These are the attributes that we

must walk in if we hope to see God's majesty. These are the things that must grow in our hearts for us to be mighty men and women in the Spirit. Innocence is at the root of who we are meant to be, and must remain at the heart of who we are. Innocence must be the quality we possess when we finish our earthly walk with God. Imagine entering heaven with a higher level of innocence and wonder than when we started our journey with Him!

This is exactly what we are called to do as Christians, as the Apostle Peter made clear in 1 Peter 3:8–17:

Finally, all of you be of one mind, having compassion for one another; love as brothers, be tenderhearted, be courteous; not returning evil for evil or reviling for reviling, but on the contrary blessing, knowing that you were called to this, that you may inherit a blessing. For

"He who would love life
And see good days,
Let him refrain his tongue from evil,
And his lips from speaking deceit.
Let him turn away from evil and do good;
Let him seek peace and pursue it.
For the eyes of the LORD are on the righteous,
And His ears are open to their prayers;
But the face of the LORD is against those who do evil."

And who is he who will harm you if you become
followers of what is good? But even if you should
suffer for righteousness' sake, you are blessed. "And
do not be afraid of their threats, nor be troubled."
But sanctify the Lord God in your hearts, and always
be ready to give a defense to everyone who asks you
a reason for the hope that is in you, with meekness
and fear; having a good conscience, that when they
defame you as evildoers, those who revile your good
conduct in Christ may be ashamed. For it is better, if
it is the will of God, to suffer for doing good than for
doing evil.

This entire passage is about the role of innocence and
purity in a Christian's life. Peter outlined exactly what
innocence looks like: being harmonious with others,
sympathetic, brotherly, kindhearted, humble in spirit,
not returning evil for evil, and not trading insult for
insult. We were called to be a blessing to others.

Many people live without thinking. They could put
the whole of their philosophy of being on a pinhead and
still have room enough for two angels to waltz.

What comes out of our mouths in non-control
situations is always the unconquered part of our nature.
Concepts such as love, agreement, compassion and
humility can only be birthed through the head and the
heart combining. This is the heart of meditation. We give
ourselves a phenomenal chance of success when head

and heart work through the issues of life and arrive at a way of seeing, speaking and being before the crises of life may happen. Such mental and emotional activity creates values.

Values are the road map of our spirituality. Our objective is to avoid retaliation, sarcasm, anger, bitterness and resentment. These reactions are soulish and keep us tied to the flesh. A value is a predetermined way of thinking that guides our words and actions in the heat of the moment. Spiritual people are ready for life in all its forms. They are not caught napping. They train themselves in Godliness by combining head and heart with the fruit of the Spirit. The best way to manifest love, joy, peace, patience, kindness, goodness, faithfulness, gentleness and self-control is by thoughtful passion.

We are our own best case study. Examining the history of our relationships is incredibly important. Thinking back through the times of our disappointments, arguments and differences of opinion is crucial to development. In hindsight what would we change about what we said or did? How would we change it?

> Meditation on your past produces wisdom for the future.

Relationships are full of highs and lows. How can we make the highs more memorable and the lows more loving and generous? Failure to learn from our mistakes means we are doomed to repeat them.

It is an important part of our growth in Christ that we retrace our steps to areas of defeat, rejection and disillusionment to deliberately work out a better resolution in our own heart for ourselves. Leave this response there and return to the present. The next time a similar situation occurs, our behavior has a better option to choose than the one that has usually resided there.

It is called imprinting or repatterning. Erasing an old way of thinking and replacing it with something new. Repentance is crucial to breakthrough. It means to think again, think in a different way, literally to change your mindset. Jesus is always our example and our sponsor in terms of how to live this kingdom life. He is the pattern that God is making in our lives. We have His imprint and we are His stamp upon humanity. A stamp is an object that has been impressed and imprinted with a design. It is a characteristic mark that identifies the maker. As Jesus is our example, mark, stamp and pattern, then our lifestyle and behavior is an exhibit of His essential nature. When we exhibit the Savior we also are impacted by the favor that rests upon such a lifestyle. (See 1 Timothy 1:16; 4:12; Titus 2:7; Hebrews 8:5; 1 Peter 2:20, 21.)

All behavior needs training. Unchecked we all revert to how we normally manifest ourselves. By deleting our old file and starting a better one we develop wisdom by the power of the Spirit.

There is always a better way to live. Scripture calls it a more excellent way. We overcome evil with good. The goodness that overwhelms must be thought through, rehearsed, before it is required. Our new nature in Christ must be nurtured by the Spirit and established through meditation and spiritual discipline. We cannot be stopped if our intention is continuous good. Everything falls to the goodness of God in a yielded life. We are called to inherit a blessing and to be a benediction to the whosoever.

Heaven is a place full of blessing that can never run out. It is eternally replenished by the nature of God. Heaven is fullness exemplified. When we say "on earth as it is in heaven", we position our attitude into expectancy. To recreate heaven's largesse on earth must be our dream. If every Christian were to challenge heaven by giving, the church would be revived and the world a better place. The world is bad, not because of the wickedness it contains, but because too few Christians really believe in the power of goodness.

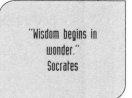

"Wisdom begins in wonder."
Socrates

The world's need for manifested goodness, and our destiny to be a blessing, are inextricably linked. Our double-mindedness on this has helped to create an unstable world.

I am always saddened to see the Church stand in judgment against the world. We are here to give a blessing – not a sentence. I think many believers and churches do not have a right theology of judgment.

There is only one Judge, and it is not the church. Judgment, mercy and grace are not acts of God, they are attributes of God. It's the overflow of who God is, He is a God of judgment, and He is the Judge. He is also a God of mercy whose people must show mercy. He is a God of grace who has called His church to be gracious. Grace, mercy and judgment; how do we hold these disparate things together? They are all the character of God and we hold them in tension in our relationship with Him. We read in Hebrews 4:16 (NASB):

> *"Therefore let us draw near with confidence to the throne of grace, so that we may receive mercy and find grace to help in time of need."*

The throne of grace is the place of undisputed power and authority. The place of authority and judgment is also the place of grace and mercy. When we come to His throne we must not come in fear or trembling but with confidence. Judgment is a sober assessment of something or someone. When we come to God we come to One who knows all truth. Only the truth He sees about us and about His provision for us can actually set us free. Before we can perceive of our need for salvation, we must first have a sober assessment of our life and our inability to be free of sin. That is judgment in its kindest form. A critique of our behavior and a firm pointing to the all-sufficiency of God's grace and mercy on our behalf.

The Cross is judgment and sentence combined. God judged Jesus on our behalf and sentenced Him to separation from His Presence through death. Now, as we come to the Cross, we are judged but not punished. We receive grace and mercy in abundance. Now we are taught to be confident in the grace and mercy of God.

It is the role of the Holy Spirit to make us feel bad when we are bad. Conviction of sin is not followed by condemnation, but by grace and mercy. Condemnation keeps us from forgiveness. It prevents us from approaching God. Condemnation leads us to shame. Conviction leads us to the throne of grace where we will find mercy to help us to grow and change.

We come to a God who makes a sober assessment of His people. A God who critiques political systems and personal behavior. We come to a God who assesses morality and appraises us as we seek to shape up to being a people of justice.

But we also come to a God who is overflowing with grace and mercy. The One who has everlasting patience and kindness. A God of love who is eternally good.

It is the throne of grace that authenticates our ministry. Judgment enables us to understand the depth of grace and mercy that is required. A sober assessment of something or someone enables us to comprehend the measure of kindness and love that must be applied. It brings us to reality and enables us to realistically engage the proper means of support that we must bring to a person or situation.

Jesus has been judged at Calvary so that all who come to Him in life will receive grace and mercy. The Day of Judgment occurs at the end of all things, where God will open His books and take His place as Judge. Between those two dates we live in a prophetic season of grace where the church exists to represent the mercy of God.

In the course of life people will reap what they sow physically, emotionally and also legally through the judicial system.

Our commission is to embrace grace and mercy. We may have some strong things to say at times. As ambassadors we may have to make an assessment on behalf of God. This assessment, though, has two elements. Firstly, a sober assessment of the condition of a person in truth; secondly, an assessment of how much grace, mercy and love must be applied so that the truth of who God wants to be for them can set them free from the law of sin and death.

To properly understand the use of judgment and grace together, we must apply them in our own lives first. Paul writes: *"Let him who thinks he stands take heed lest he fall"* (1 Corinthians 10:12). Peter speaks of the need for diligence in faith, moral excellence, knowledge, self-control, perseverance, godliness, brotherly kindness and love: *"For if these qualities are yours and are increasing, they render you neither useless nor unfruitful in the true knowledge of our Lord Jesus Christ"* (2 Peter 1:8, NASB).

On no account must we stand in judgment of others when our own lives cannot stand scrutiny. Jesus' words: *"Do not judge so that you will not be judged"* (Matthew 7:1, NASB), is common sense for the spiritual. Judgment attracts judgment. *"For in the way you judge, you will be judged"* (Matthew 7:2, NASB). For a Christian, judgment is the sober assessment of another's condition in order to reveal to them the grace, mercy, goodness and kindness of God that can lead to repentance and a changed life. As ambassadors of God who stand before the throne of grace ourselves, we speak as much from our own testimony as a witness of God's great mercy. This type of judgment attracts repentance because it glorifies God.

Christendom is called to give the earth a taste of what heaven will be like. If more Christians would stand up in the goodness of God, acting it out in every facet of their lives, society would be changed immeasurably.

We should see more than just tiny pockets of innocence in the Church. One of my great friends, a person who has prayed for my ministry for more than twenty-five years, continually challenges me with her strong example of Christian innocence. Twenty years ago, someone in a home group meeting turned on her and snapped: "The problem with you is you're so naïve!" She was absolutely crushed. But I told her that it was good to be naïve. She has an innocent quality to her. She viewed God with an incredible sense of wonder. Her purity caused the other person's cynicism to surface; she had shone light on the darkness of their own heart. This person had tried to squash in her the very thing that they needed.

Jesus' sense of wonder

Jesus, however, never squashed anyone's righteousness; on the contrary, His own sense of wonder surfaced when He saw others who walked in innocence and purity. One of the few times Jesus said "behold" – or, as we would term it, "wow" – was when He first met Nathanael, a man who later became one of His disciples. *"Behold an Israelite indeed, in whom is no guile!"* Jesus exclaimed in John 1:47 (KJV).

What did Jesus see in Nathanael? He saw a man without deceit. The Message version of the Bible translates Jesus as saying, *"There's a real Israelite, not a false bone in his body."* Jesus saw his innocence and loved it.

Innocence is a quality we are born with and then slowly lose through the experiences of our life. Every time we have one of those bitter experiences, as we call them, a part of our purity erodes away. The way we think and perceive things in the spirit withers as we become guarded, wary, mistrustful, and suspicious. When another bitter experience occurs in our life, another layer of grime is placed on our sense of wonder. Given enough time, we become unsure that we were ever innocent. Meanwhile, we look at everyone around us and see the worst.

The most important "felt" needs in every person are the need to be loved, to belong, and to be significant. Every relationship therefore must be concerned with the acts of treasuring, protecting and nurturing.

This is love in its truest form. The Father gives us worth in the Son. He declares our value. We are honored by His Presence. He shows us His unfathomable riches in Christ, but also affirms that we are His riches. Peter describes us as: "His special treasure" (1 Peter 2:9).

- Everyone loves to be treasured
- Wonder connects us with the experience of God's love
- Treasuring, protecting and nurturing are key elements in building relationships!

He is our refuge, fortress and high tower. He sets our feet upon a rock, lifting us above our enemies. His Word and Spirit combine to teach us power and authority. He protects the flock.

He nurtures us like children. He causes the growth of His tender young plants (1 Corinthians 3:6, 7). He gives us the nourishment of His Presence. He disciples us vertically, one on one, by His Spirit, and also horizontally, through His chosen people. Our commission is to make disciples, literally to enable people to grow up in all things in Christ (Ephesians 4:11–16).

We must produce a body that is capable of more than just membership and function. It must also become the Bride; the One cherished by the One; full of love, laughter, grace and beauty.

These attributes and more are only gained through right relationships. It requires a relational paradigm to produce the Bride of Christ. Gift, ministry, vision and calling will enable us to do *"greater works than these"* (John 14:12).

But the Bride cannot be produced by function only. She requires an environment of deepest love, true committed friendships and a community where love, grace, mercy, kindness, joy, peace, patience, goodness, faithfulness and gentleness are all actively sought and encouraged as a way of life.

The only deliberate, intentional way to attract and keep the Presence of the Holy Spirit is to choose the fruit of His Nature (Galatians 5:22–26), ahead of the power of His giftedness. Again, the issue between character and gift is primary. We value both, but which is most needful? To live by the Spirit we must embrace the Nature of God.

To move in the supernatural realm, we must allow His giftings free reign in our calling. The Bride is the fruit of the Spirit working in committed relationships.

Deep, dynamic love that is unselfish and empowering delivers us to a place of simplicity and wonder. To know beyond all doubt that we are accepted and loved in such a glorious manner releases an understanding about love that is captivating and full of enchantment.

To understand and experience love at depth is so transforming to our confidence. We belong to a loving Father who will nurture us constantly through His faithfulness.

Jesus, the same Man who saw and loved Nathanael's purity, also allowed Judas Iscariot to be close to Him. Jesus' own sense of wonder about who God was allowed Him to be true to Himself and love the unlovely. He was a friend to sinners without being tainted by them.

The modern-day Church appears to have downgraded this function. While the early Church was full of pioneers for change, the current Church is a refuge from it. Around the world, Christians are taught to not mix with the world. Misinterpreted phrases like "unequally yoked" and "in the world but not of the world" are thrown from pulpits, causing Christians to forsake any pre-Christian friends. What nonsense! Our role is to be in the earth, touching as many people as we can with the love and purity and hope of Christ. We touch them, but are not touched by what they are into. I believe that if Jesus returned tomorrow, He would build a community of grace in the red-light district and begin talking with drunks, prostitutes, the abused, and the other marginalized members of society. He would go to the gay community. He would hang out in the slummiest bars in town. He would march boldly into the places the

Church is deathly afraid to tread. Ever since Jesus turned water into wine, evangelicals have been trying to change it back. The church is not confident in the overcoming power of God. The purity of God is a powerful weapon against darkness. The quality of our innocence in the Spirit is protection enough.

> "If a child is to keep his inborn sense of wonder, he needs the companionship of at least one adult who can share it, rediscovering with him the joy, excitement and mystery of the world we live in."
> Rachel Carson

Innocence is always under the threat of attack. But purity isn't about what others can do to us, it's about who we want to be. We can remain pure in heart and remain watchful for unscrupulous and disrespectful people at the same time.

We are in control of our own sense of wonder. Jesus dealt with this idea when, in Mark 7:6, He defined what He considered hypocrisy to be: *"This people honors Me with their lips, but their heart is far from Me."* When our hearts are bitter, hard, callous, unfeeling, cynical, judgmental, angry, suspicious, closed, wary, distrustful, jealous, skeptical, derisive, contemptuous, pessimistic, unbelieving, sarcastic, or scornful, we hurt ourselves – these things are corrosive to innocence. The damage we do to our own purity is far greater than the damage we can inflict on anyone else's. Giving in to impurity grieves the Spirit of God. Our hardness grows as we protect ourselves from people and situations. We get hurt and we swear an unholy vow: "I'll never let that happen to me again." Immediately, we begin to insulate our hearts from taking another chance on someone or something. We close ourselves off relationally.

As we can see from Luke 9:46–48, Jesus always knew what people were feeling in their hearts:

> *Then a dispute arose among them as to which of them would be greatest. And Jesus, perceiving the thought of their heart, took a little child and set him by Him, and said to them, "Whoever receives this little child in My name receives Me; and whoever receives Me receives Him who sent Me. For he who is least among you all will be great."*

Unless we become child-like in innocence and purity, we won't be able to see the wonders God wants to show us. Jesus wanted us to throw away our pride and self-protectionism and live a truly spiritual life.

In another setting, Jesus exposed the darkness in the hearts of the religious leaders of His day. In Matthew 9, Jesus looked at a paralytic and said: *"Son, be of good cheer; your sins are forgiven you."* The man got up and walked. But instead of rejoicing over God's power, the Pharisees and scribes who witnessed the healing were enraged: *"And at once some of the scribes said within themselves, 'This Man blasphemes!'"* Jesus knew His statement would get a reaction, but He wanted to expose the bitterness of their hearts. *"But Jesus, knowing their thoughts, said, 'Why do you think evil in your hearts?'"*

Their judgmental attitude was a product of their own sin – not Jesus' provocative words of healing.

diversity and conformity

The key to wonder and its joys and delights, is to understand the paradox between being in Christ in the Spirit and being the person that God created you to be in the natural.

We are individuals called to be in fellowship with a company of called-out people. We must celebrate our uniqueness and understand the particular contribution we are designed to make.

As a community of believers in a specific location, we value the diversity of gift, calling, ministry and destiny upon each life. We also must celebrate our conformity to the character of God by choosing to live out from a set of values that include the nature of God, the fruit of the Spirit, and the life of Christ. Godhead relationships must be a real place of fellowship where we all become Christ-like.

Diversity in our gift and mission must be under-girded by conformity in character and lifestyle. What a great paradox! Failure to live in the necessary tension between those extremes will cause our ministry to be discontinued, our fellowship to split and Jesus to be dishonored.

Who am I in Christ? What was I created to become in the womb? David states this in Psalm 139:13–18:

For You formed my inward parts;
You covered me in my mother's womb.
I will praise You, for I am fearfully and wonderfully
       made;
Marvelous arc Your works,
And that my soul knows very well.
My frame was not hidden from You,
When I was made in secret,
And skillfully wrought in the lowest parts of the
       earth.
Your eyes saw my substance, being yet unformed.
And in Your book they all were written,
The days fashioned for me,
When as yet there were none of them.
How precious also are Your thoughts to me, O God!
How great is the sum of them!
If I should count them, they would be more in
       number than the sand;
When I awake, I am still with You!

We serve a God who does all things well. Everything He made was "good". That includes you and me.

Salvation is not just about gaining freedom from the past, to live well in the present and prepare for the future. It is also about the recovery of our primary identity. If indeed I am fearfully and wonderfully made, then I cannot despise myself. Instead I must come to understand my body, how my mind functions, and the elements of my personality. We are all unique in some way. Similarities obviously will exist between people. To celebrate someone's uniqueness is the height of friendship. To know the people whom God has put around you, how they tick, and what their contribution is to your life, is vital. God knows us inside out and we must know ourselves.

I am an introvert. I love my personality. I'm quiet, shy, introspective. In Christ, under the anointing, I become more of an extrovert (by comparison). I am powerfully persuasive, often quite funny and very incisive when the Holy Spirit is moving. My memory is poor. I have trained myself to take notes in a particular way. I am not a good organizer. The Lord gave me Carole, my personal assistant for over twenty years. My body requires more exercise than most. There are certain foods that while tasting great are not a blessing in reality. My weight oscillates between exercise (or lack of it), travel, time zones, cultures and available food groups around the hemispheres. My schedule takes its toll, and it's important for me to laugh at that. My weight does not detract from who I am. On some days there might just be a little more of me available! I'm comfortable in my skin.

I need stillness. I love to meditate. I love my friends. I am a thinker, so renewing my mind in the spirit makes me incredibly happy. I love revelation so I adore the Spirit of Truth. He makes me worship.

One of my main contributions to the life of my friends is my capacity for deep thought. I love mentoring. I love the prophetic. I am so excited about all the possibilities of what God may do next. I see the next phase of inheritance in people. I love turning people on to the Nature of God; what He is *really* like; and what He wants to be next for people as their relationship with Him grows. Our view of God always requires an upgrade to enable us to see who we are going to become in the next season.

My ministry on one level is to reach Christians for Christ. I work with people who want to break through boundaries in themselves. People who want supernatural experiences and who are looking for a greater meaning in life.

I work with organizations, sacred and secular, to understand that destiny can only be achieved by accessing the spiritual realm. All of life is spiritual. I enable them to develop a greater corporate capacity for expansion by empowering and releasing the unique contribution of the individual.

The Pharisees were the dream thieves of their day. They developed a system that overrode individuality. They had a set of external rules that killed creativity. They made people conform to a practice instead of a character. They robbed people of intuition and being led by the Spirit. The system they spawned enabled them to maintain control in their own authority and status. This was the prison door that Jesus came to open (Luke 4:18–21). This was the oppression He came to deliver God's people from … the leaven of the Pharisees. The church leaders of His day were far more oppressive than the Romans.

The only form of control that is acceptable in church life is the fruit of self-control. To teach people how to govern their own lives through accountability within good, honest, loving relationships.

- Celebrate your uniqueness
- Real diversity requires authentic conformity
- Salvation is concerned with the recovery of our prime identity
- The Pharisees were the dream thieves of their day
- Personal development is linked to wonder
- Character is the soil of spirituality; gifting is the seed.

Personal development must link people to wonder. To love who they were created to be and to get back to that place of identity and gratitude. Then see that identity become more embellished as we put on Christ. Our sinfulness in abeyance through the Cross, our real self in Christ being revealed by the Holy Spirit.

Do not try to be someone else. Do not wish your life away. You are fearfully and wonderfully made. Allow the Holy Spirit to enable you to recover your identity and help you to discover your place of fit within the company of friends where your salvation is worked out in the Spirit.

The core of our spirituality is built on relationship, not function. We were created to be, and then were called to do. We cannot understand our life outside of what it is that we get to "be" for people around us. The moment we define our life as a function, we are demonstrating that we do not have a relationship that enables us to discover our true self.

I am a peaceful, tranquil man. I love kindness. My patience rules in circumstances. Gentleness disarms people. I see beyond potential. I am wise because I understand many of the ways of God. The Father is with me, I am learning to be with Him. I am an enigma who inspires people to love God more.

In my function, I am an architect and builder. I am a warrior excited by the opposition. I am a strategist, a teacher who is prophetic. I love to give financially. I love excellence and dislike mediocrity. I will not settle for less; I am stubborn in this regard.

Of course, that is not the sum total of who I am. It is a synopsis. It all comes through the work of the Holy Spirit. Our co-operation and obedience shape our identity, which will determine our destiny. Character is the soil of spirituality and our gifting is the seed. Make sure the ground of your life is honorable. It is possible to destroy with our character what God has built through our gift.

Dependency and wonder are the keys to maintaining and enjoying a true depth of spirituality.

the good news

The scribes had completely lost their sense of wonder and filtered everything through the lens of their own bitter experiences. Many of us are in a similar state today, unable to see the miracles of God because of our own lens of disappointment.

I believe that the goal of God is to make sure happiness touches us no matter what is occurring. Heaven, from what I read of Scripture, is full of light, laughter, love and joy. God is the King of love. Jesus came so that our joy would be full.

If we truly believe God is completely counter-culture, the total antithesis of the world, then He must be joyful! The gospel is so incredible, it's almost too good to be true. It's so outrageous that it's almost fantasy. God's grace and love should boggle our minds: it's a dream come true.

"From without, no wonderful effect is wrought within ourselves, unless some interior, responding wonder meets it."
Herman Melville

Why won't we let His goodness affect our hearts? God wants to bless us again and again, and see that blessing spill over from us on to other people. When He blesses us, He is actually blessing the crowd of people around us, for our friends, family and neighbors can't help but share our lives and excitement.

What if having a sense of wonder was as easy as being awed by what God is doing in our life? Shouldn't His grace lift our heart? Shouldn't our spirit be vibrating with excitement at the thought of how God is working? What if we let go of the cynicism of the world around us? God has so much for each of us that, even if we lived to be 120 years old, we wouldn't scratch the surface of His goodness.

Children have an uncomplicated trust. God is marvelous, and we must accept that in order to be child-like and see His Kingdom flourish around us. To be healthy, we must stay in the fruit of the Spirit – love, joy, peace, longsuffering, kindness, goodness, faithfulness, gentleness, self-control – and live in the presence of God.

fiery trials

In theory, we would all love to remain pure and innocent when we face difficult issues and situations. In practice, doing so is difficult – but not impossible. Throughout the Bible, we read of men and women of God overcoming awful tribulations. How did they do it? The Apostle Peter, one of those people who could have chosen to look at the world through bitter eyes but didn't, offered this advice in 1 Peter 4:12–16:

> *Beloved, do not think it strange concerning the fiery trial which is to try you, as though some strange thing happened to you; but rejoice to the extent that you partake of Christ's sufferings, that when His glory is revealed, you may also be glad with exceeding joy. If you are reproached for the name of Christ, blessed are you, for the Spirit of glory and of*

God rests upon you. On their part He is blasphemed,
but on your part He is glorified. But let none of you
suffer as a murderer, a thief, an evildoer, or as a
busybody in other people's matters. Yet if anyone
suffers as a Christian, let him not be ashamed, but
let him glorify God in this matter.

I know of people who have been locked away in a
communist gulag for years. Their partners and children
have been abducted by the state. They have endured
absolutely inhuman treatment, slave labor, violence,
torture, solitary confinement, starvation, and their hair,
teeth and finger nails pulled out.

One man was locked into a coffin with nails in it for
days on end. Another was dropped up to his chin in a
cesspool of human waste. There are other magnificent
stories of people standing before firing squads where the
guns would misfire when pointed at them, but otherwise
worked fine!

One man in solitary confinement for months on end
tapped out the gospel in Morse code on the waste pipe in
his cell; dozens of people were converted. One such
person was Richard Wurmbrand who I was immensely
privileged to meet many years ago. This man suffered
abominably at the hands of the communists for over two
decades in prison. I have never seen a more gracious,
kind or happier man. That meeting still profoundly
affects me years later. Richard knew God.

I have been privileged to speak to several such people. They all have one thing in common – a sense of wonder and joy in the Lord. They never saw prison as a punishment, only as an opportunity to work in a parish nobody else wanted. One such ex-prisoner told me, "If your freedom is truly internal, then you are free no matter where you are or what is happening."

These people walked through their fiery trial with their innocence and purity enlarged, not diminished.

wonder and security

We live in the midst of the clash of two kingdoms. Warfare is often fierce and bitter. This is not a "made for TV" type of warfare. It is unrelenting, hideous, full of malice and spite, accusatory, vindictive, physical, mental, intimidatory. Fear is a major key for the enemy. Many times the first words uttered when God shows up are, "do not fear".

Peace

Rest is a weapon. To know peace at depth is a most urgent discipline to acquire. To be able to bring yourself to peace in moments under severe pressure is vital.

Living in the Spirit is about knowing your position in Christ: to know the real difference between your state, i.e. how you see yourself in the natural (usually a negative and inferior perspective), and your standing, i.e. your personal revelation of how you see yourself by the Spirit (in Christ, in the body, in favor, etc.).

The Holy Spirit promotes the reality of who you are in Christ at every opportunity. He renews your mind to transform your spirituality. He leads you into all truth so that you become accustomed to breaking through into a place of fullness.

In warfare especially, there is a place that the Spirit would take us to that would open up the reality of being "In Christ" to a vastly different degree than our evangelical "norm".

God has always been the Rock, the fortress, the refuge, the hiding place for His people. There is no greater security than His Presence. In warfare, there are attributes of God to both experience and acquire. Love casts out fear; peace overrules anxiety; intimacy subdues intimidation; purity humbles accusation; truth conquers lies.

- Wonder is built upon a convinced sense of our security in God
- Life in the Spirit is about state and standing
- The real battle is always for intimacy, not territory
- People without Presence are not a threat to the enemy

The real battle is always for intimacy, not territory. The enemy will lure us into a fight over geography before we are ready for it. Warfare is first relational, like everything else. We stand against the enemy by being in the Presence of God. Warfare is about discovering all that God is to us in His majesty, sovereignty and supremacy.

Security in God is essential. Being able to retreat into Him is vital. Proverbs 18:10 states: *"The Name of the LORD is a strong tower; the righteous run to it and are safe."*

Before we go marching out against our adversary, we must first go boldly into the Presence of God. Worship is the key to successful warfare. Our intimacy intimidates our foe.

We must not only feel safe, we must expect it. Confidence in God's desire and ability to protect must reach the place of wonder. God has conquered both life and death, so that we fear nothing. Paul writes in 1 Corinthians 15:55: *"Death, where is your sting?"*

[handwritten margin notes: fear in childbirth, God can overcome that fear & replace it w/ peace & rest]

I love my life; I'm also looking forward to dying. It's the last great adventure, to cross over to the place where everything is clear. How marvelous to see God, to be full of wonder and astonishment for eternity!

I'm so excited about making that journey, when it's my time. I want to run towards death and take a leap. I'm ready now. Until that great day arrives, I want to make each day count towards the glory of God.

I love my life and I love the security of being wrapped up in Christ. Security in God must be drawn into a place of wonder so that the confidence that wonder creates may be significant on the battlefield. If we are going to slay a thousand, we need a sense of wonder. Without it we may never even slay one enemy.

We are not looking for the enemy. We are seekers of God. When we find Him in abundance, the enemy will come looking for us. People without Presence are not a threat to the enemy. They are easily disheartened and subdued.

Those whom God inhabits fully are always singled out by the principalities and powers. There is a place in the Spirit set aside for us where no weapon can prosper against us. We can make the enemy tired, weary and inferior through the quality of our rest and peace. We cannot be intimidated because we are too busy being fascinated . . . by Jesus.

It is vital to know how to abide in the vine, to dwell and remain in Christ. The enemy seeks to draw us out of what God has put us in . . . Christ. The Holy Spirit seeks to establish us in Christ and open up new places in the Spirit through intimacy. David writes in the Psalms of how it is intimacy that reveals the true nature of the God who laughs at His enemies (Psalm 2:1–4; 37:12–15).

Our sense of wonder in God's supremacy is our confidence and our victory. It kills our passivity and enables us to act whilst the enemy is raging. Our heart remains in rest. Assurance comes out of our wonder.

"All who desire to live godly in Christ Jesus will suffer persecution."
The Apostle Paul

"All who desire to live godly in Christ Jesus will suffer persecution" (NASB), Paul told Timothy in 2 Timothy 3:12. The problem with the western Church is that we're not good enough for the enemy to be bothered oppressing us. We are insignificant so there's no need for persecution. Why bother attacking something that's irrelevant?

Because of this lack of persecution, we miss out on a doorway to increased blessing. Peter writes in 1 Peter

4:14 (NASB), *"If you are reviled for the name of Christ, you are blessed, because the spirit of glory and of God rests on you."* At all times our face is towards the fullness of Who God is for us. David writes in Psalm 34:5: *"They looked to Him and were radiant."*

It is this Spirit-promoted ability to see the Lord in all things that keeps our heart tuned to His glorious nature. A sense of wonder about God can help us move beyond the pain of persecution and into a deeper place in the Spirit. *"Blessed are those who are persecuted for righteousness' sake, for theirs is the kingdom of heaven,"* Jesus said in Matthew 5:10.

> "If you want to be happy, be."
> Leo Tolstoy

Something glorious rested on those suffering believers in communist prisons. It was wonderful to see it. They had reached a place in the Spirit where they were more sensitive to Christ than they were to the persecution they experienced.

Fiery trials don't have to be persecution. In Africa, poverty is just as powerful as persecution. I love visiting Africa because the only way people can live is by the power of a miracle. They have nothing and no means of getting anything. That's why more miracles happen in Africa than in the western world. While we have good hygiene, clean water, abundant food, and sturdy homes, they have nothing but miracles to survive on.

In every home I visited in Africa, I would pray over their food store and ask God to never let it run out. I went back, year after year, and heard their testimonies: "Our food never runs out." One family didn't buy food for two years because, every day, the food had returned to their cupboard. I stayed there a week and I swear I ate the same fish every day. I nicknamed it "Eric." Every dinner time, Eric was back on my plate. "How are you doing, Eric?" I'd laugh. "Nice to eat you again."

Africa doesn't need our money, they need miracles. They pray for their water supply, their health, their children. I always know what God wants to do out there: miracles, miracles, miracles, miracles. By praying that a family would never be ill, they become a testimony to their friends and acquaintances. They become living signs and wonders. Their lives become so powerful and outrageous that they carry divine significance to the people around them.

It is interesting to note that when Africans depend upon western money, the flow of miracles can be small and the people diminished in spirit. Dependency aids the supernatural. The number of churches in Africa that are truly supernatural is growing. They not only have miracles, they have money. They live in an expectation of abundance and are not tied to their external circumstances. Their experience of Word and Spirit transcends the natural world, creating a different state of order.

Western Christians are now coming to Africa to receive. Africans know how to live under an open heaven. Western believers are coming under the anointing of dependency and wonder as Africans praise and pray down their inheritance.

Word and Spirit are not dependent on the earth's economy. Dependency and wonder opens windows in heaven and floods the earth with the abundance of God. It transforms locations. It is what the ancient Celtic Christians call "a thin place", where heaven meets earth. Western believers should invest in such places and learn from the anointing that resides there.

the joy of dependency

God expects us to love and give freely, because He Himself loves and gives freely. In Romans 11:35, the Apostle Paul marvels at this quality: *"Or who has first given to Him and it shall be repaid to him?"* The answer is no one, Paul says in verse 36: *"For of Him and through Him and to Him are all things, to whom be glory forever."*

This is the true circle of life, as Disney's *Lion King* would say. Nothing we give to God originates in ourselves. Instead, we give to Him that which He has already deposited in us. Something comes from God and is put into our lives, and we give it back to Him in a variety of ways. God gives these gifts to the Christ that is within us. Only Jesus gives us the opportunity to have a relationship with God. *"To them God willed to make known what are the riches of the glory of this mystery among the Gentiles: which is Christ in you, the hope of glory,"* Paul wrote in Colossians 1:27. This is the true prosperity gospel ... *"Christ in you, the hope of glory."* Because Christ lives in us, we can be certain of God's provision in our lives.

Everything God wants from us will be given to us first. He never demands something of us unless He has already deposited it in us through Christ. Any revelation we have is given by God in the first place. Any worship we give Him was placed in us by Him. Any love we offer Him exists

> "Blessed are those who hunger and thirst for righteousness, for they shall be filled."
> Jesus Christ

because He first loved us. Any glory given to God came from Him in the first place. We simply return to God the very thing He has already given us.

Living this way in the Spirit is an instinctive and intuitive thing. When we have the joy of dependency, we can live expectantly. No Christian should ever be intimidated by life; we should be too busy being fascinated by Jesus.

I want to live an expectant life. I'm learning to be fascinated by God and what He is doing, not intimidated by the circumstances swirling around me. I want to look for God in the day-to-day issues of my life. He is the One who smiles and says in Jeremiah 29:11 (NASB): *"I know the plans that I have for you ... plans for welfare and not for calamity to give you a future and a hope."* I know that God is up to something every moment of every day, and I want to be a part of that plan. What is it about my current situation that God wants to use to show me more of His nature? I want to embrace the principle of Romans 8:28 – *"And we know that all things work together for good to those who love God, to those who are the called according to His purpose."*

When we live in child-like simplicity, there is nothing that can overcome us. *"We are more than conquerors through Him who loved us,"* Paul said in Romans 8:37. Being a conqueror isn't just about one person being free; it's about setting others free to live the same lifestyle we do.

Thanksgiving and thankfulness are essential to wonder. We must celebrate our freedom continuously. Paul writes to the Galatians *"It was for freedom that Christ set us free"* (Galatians 5:1, NASB). The word "free" in Greek is *gratis*, from where we obtain the word "gratitude".

> Thanksgiving and gratitude are both essential to wonder.

Gratitude is the attitude of being free, and giving of thanks is the expression of that in word form.

The price God paid can never be reimbursed. For that we are grateful. Gratefulness is paradoxical too, in that it has an immediate and spontaneous expression. It is best seen in an emotional context of exuberance and spontaneous delight. This is usually event-driven and circumstantial, and does not remain beyond a certain season or timeframe.

The other side of the paradox is that gratitude, linked to real internal change, remains as a lifelong expression of thanks. When transformation occurs, we become more intimate with the person of God. What He does is wonderful, but Who He is, is marvelous.

When our understanding of the nature of God is upgraded, so is our thanksgiving and our sense of wonder. God is the gift and the ultimate benefit. G.K. Chesterton wrote: "To be thankful is the highest form of thought and gratitude is happiness doubled by wonder."

What would be the opposite of thankfulness and gratitude, and where would that take us in our relationship with the Father? No-one is intentionally ungrateful; we become that by default. Plan to upgrade your gratitude and see where that takes you in terms of developing a sense of wonder.

> "Blessed are the pure in heart, for they shall see God."
> Jesus Christ

The worst thing we can do for a pre-Christian is to only try to evangelize them. I don't think God ever just asks us to evangelize anyone. He asks us to be His witness. A witness to what He is really like, a representative of the Most High.

We do this best by our lifestyle, not our words. A lifestyle of loving God outrageously opens the hearts of all we meet. A lifestyle of being unafraid, generous, happy, peaceful, loving and kind will explode everyone's perception of God. We lead people to His nature so that salvation is a formality, not a battle of wits.

I do think that God asks us to live in such a way that people around us are intrigued by His nature. And I think we must be ready with an answer when they ask us about what they perceive about us and God. We must look constantly for what God is doing and walk with that plan. This was how Jesus shared the love of God, as He explained in John 5:19: *"Most assuredly, I say to you, the Son can do nothing of Himself, but what He sees the Father do; for whatever He does, the Son also does in like manner."*

When God points a person out and tells us to do or say something specifically to them, He's already given us what we're about to give away. What He has given us is meant to be a gift to that person. And what goes back to God is that person's changed heart and our obedience. *"Freely you have received, freely give,"* Jesus said in Matthew 10:8. Evangelism is about being part of the cycle that God wants to initiate in someone else's life.

The joy of dependency is knowing that no situation can stop God from working in us. *"No weapon formed against you shall prosper,"* says Isaiah 54:17. God's power in us can overcome anything, all by itself. When we see God as big as He really is, when we are filled with a sense of wonder, and when we are child-like, we see ourselves the way God sees us: as an unstoppable force for good.

The Godhead is the blueprint for life and committed friendships. God is in a relationship with Himself. He loves Himself with all of His being. The Father loves the Son and gives Him center stage at His baptism, saying in Luke 3:22, *"You are My Beloved Son; in You I am well pleased."* He steps into the wings to honor and prefer Jesus.

Jesus only ever points to His Father. John 5:30 records His statement: *"I can of Myself do nothing . . . I do not seek My own will but the will of the Father who sent Me."* Later, in John 16:7, 13, 14, Jesus makes this remarkable statement:

> *"It is to your advantage that I go away; for if I do not go away, the Helper will not come to you. But if I depart, I will send Him to you . . . When He . . . has come, He will guide you into all truth . . . He will glorify Me, for He will take of what is Mine and declare it to you."*

The Holy Spirit only wants to talk about Christ, and reveal His person to the Church, establishing us in Christ. A perfect model of relationship and partnership, full of mutual love, honor, commitment and service. They only cared for one another, and wanted each other to succeed and be much glorified.

It is important that we at least imitate the Godhead in our relationships. We must carry the love of God for us into the realm of awe and wonder, to be amazed and astonished at being loved at such great depth. The depth of our wonder in such a matter will reveal the heights to which our own agape love can flourish in the hearts of men.

Our sense of astonishment and wonder at God's love personally is the catalyst for us to partner with the Holy Spirit in developing loving relationships that overcome all obstacles, tensions and opposition. When we have been conquered by love, our own love knows no bounds. In this love our confidence is huge. We have no fear of being abused or taken for granted and used. We have more love than we need and it grows as we release it. It returns in fullness to the heart that gave it fully.

Great love always has cost attached. Someone must pay a price to release love. It is imperative, therefore, that we see God's love as an investment in us for our own benefit. His love multiplies us.

Our love also has, when released by the Spirit, a cost to ourselves and an investment to the object of our attention/affection. Love invests itself for the benefit of the recipient, not the giver. Of course, we must reap what we sow, and our unselfishness reaps glory for God and maintains our sense of well-being in the Spirit. The greater wonder we have in the majesty of God's love, the greater our own love will become.

We will have so many opportunities to release love to friends, family and the unlovely. No person steeped in God's love can resist the urge to love others in more than words. Great love nurtures a sense of wonder. A commitment to walking in love is in itself a guarantee of developing wonder and astonishment.

faith to knowledge

We must come to know and believe the love which God has for us. In our spiritual journey, there is a point where we move from faith to knowledge. I no longer *believe* that Jesus Christ is Lord; I *know* that Jesus Christ is Lord. At that time, we don't have to try any more. We just *know* that Jesus is Lord.

Our job, every day, is to be loved by God. In the Bible, God refers to us several times as His "beloved." We must live in our awareness that we are His beloved, because we can only love Him by returning the love He has given us. *"We love Him because He first loved us,"* John wrote in 1 John 4:19. It is fitting that a disciple known as *the Beloved* has taught us this truth. During Jesus' time on earth, John had no choice but to be overwhelmed by God's love. He leaned on Jesus, and loved everything about Him. Our call is to do the same. We have to be overwhelmed by His mercy, overwhelmed by His grace, overwhelmed by His joy, overwhelmed by His peace, and overwhelmed by His glory.

> "Let your light so shine before men, that they may see your good works and glorify your Father in heaven."
> Jesus Christ

The moment our faith moves into knowledge, we are able to enter a deeper level of worship. Our ability to minister to the Lord grows. Prayer is no longer a chore, but an act of love. When faith becomes knowledge, we are able to consciously return to God everything that He has given us. The circle of life with God gains momentum.

"In this is love, not that we loved God, but that He loved us and sent His Son to be the propitiation for our sins," the beloved disciple wrote in 1 John 4:10. This is the center of our relationship with God: we were in sin, and He loved us. Why is this important? Because it proves that His love is not conditional on our performance as Christians. Instead, His love is based on His own nature. Nothing we do can make God love us less. Nothing we can do can make Him love us more! He loves us because He *is* love. Being beloved is our identity in Christ; it is the name by which God calls and accepts us. *"He made us accepted in the Beloved,"* Paul wrote in Ephesians 1:6.

Who are we? We are ones loved by Christ. As His children, we must learn to live with a radical amazement. Myself, I can't help but be amazed that I am the beloved of God. I'm from a large industrial city on a small island in a cold sea. I was brought up in a place so industrialized that birds wake up in the morning and cough. The community I lived in was at that time tough, crime-ridden and violent. And yet I am the beloved of God. If that isn't a miracle, I don't know what is.

wonder: the root of dependency

Developing a sense of wonder is a prerequisite to having the joy of dependency. The path to spiritual maturity is always through a child-like spirit where we are able to see God and know Him with a faith-filled simplicity. Jesus described this truth in Matthew 18:1–6:

> *At that time the disciples came to Jesus, saying, "Who then is greatest in the kingdom of heaven?"*
> *Then Jesus called a little child to Him, set him in the midst of them, and said, "Assuredly, I say to you, unless you are converted and become as little children, you will by no means enter the kingdom of heaven. Therefore whoever humbles himself as this little child is the greatest in the kingdom of heaven. Whoever receives one little child like this in My name receives Me.*
> *"But whoever causes one of these little ones who believe in Me to sin, it would be better for him if a millstone were hung around his neck, and he were drowned in the depth of the sea."*

The world we live in makes everything complex. But Jesus flies in the face of our culture, telling us that unless we are converted to the ways of being child-like, we can't enter the Kingdom. Unless we humble ourselves to think, speak and act this way, greatness will elude us.

During His ministry, He made everything simple – as evidenced by Matthew 22:35–39:

> *Then one of them, a lawyer, asked Him a question, testing Him, and saying, "Teacher, which is the great commandment in the law?"*
>
> *Jesus said to him, " 'You shall love the LORD your God with all your heart, with all your soul, and with all your mind.' This is the first and great commandment. And the second is like it: 'You shall love your neighbor as yourself.' On these two commandments hang all the Law and the Prophets."*

God wants us to think simply. Love Him, love the person next to us. This simplicity earths us in the truth of who God is and who God wants to be. The goal in our lives is to love God with everything we have, and to love everyone around us in exactly the same way we would like to be loved ourselves.

Love is an action. Words are not enough by themselves. They must be accompanied by an act of love. It is essential that we understand that our main contribution to the people around us is to love them in a practical way.

Our continual question, especially within the relationships that the Lord has entrusted to us, must be "What can I do?". How can we benefit them? How can we demonstrate the regular, continuous, all-embracing love of the Father? God loves to surprise us; how can we be part of His surprise to others?

Just what is God doing with my friends and neighbours? Don't you want to know? Prayer is finding out what God wants to do and asking Him to do it. Cultivate a sense of expectancy in your own heart about God manifesting His love to you. Then extend your borders to cover someone else.

There are ordinary umbrellas, and there are golfing umbrellas. The ordinary ones cover one; a golfing umbrella will cover several people. God is overshadowing us, so who else is His shadow covering? Whoever you stand next to at any given time, comes under your blessing. Whoever the Lord has connected you with in this current season, no matter how near or far geographically, are connected to the Father through you. What are the implications for their life and spirituality?

Seek clarity for the people around you. Open your eyes and stay spiritually aware. Be alert to the love and grace of God for the people in your life. Your heart is a sanctuary for other people to sense the heart of God for them. Your shade gives them enough covering from the harsh reality of life to enable them to feel peace and the pleasure of God's love.

> "Blessed are the poor in spirit, for theirs is the kingdom of heaven."
> Jesus Christ

Redemption is about recovering who we were created to be in this earth. We are called to a way of thinking, being, speaking, and acting that reflects heaven. We have to retrace our steps of maturity, becoming child-like again, to find a new beginning in the spiritual world. It is very important to God that He be trusted – He loves, when the odds are stacked against us, to be believed in. Children believe in things no matter what happens. Adults, however, spend their time tearing down anything that's too good to believe.

"Again, the kingdom of heaven is like treasure hidden in a field, which a man found and hid; and for joy over it he goes and sells all that he has and buys that field," Jesus explained in Matthew 13:44. Christians haven't bought the farm and died; we've bought the field and found God's unimaginable treasure! God has deposited treasure in each of our lives, treasure that can be joyfully recovered. Through the Holy Spirit, we can find that treasure and release it as part of God's redemptive plan. From God, to God: the circle of spiritual life continues as we share our treasure with everyone we come in contact with. It doesn't matter how much we give away: there will always be more than enough. The source – God Himself – gives us far more than we could ever give.

the source

By walking with God, we learn how the Kingdom of Heaven works. One of the spiritual world's most vital principles is that we can only ascend to God because He first descended to us. In Ephesians 4:8–10, Paul laid out this thought more clearly:

> *Therefore He says:*
>
> > *"When He ascended on high,*
> > *He led captivity captive,*
> > *And gave gifts to men."*
>
> *(Now this, "He ascended" – what does it mean but that He also first descended into the lower parts of the earth? He who descended is also the One who ascended far above all the heavens, that He might fill all things.)*

In all of His dealings, God takes the initiative. He comes down so that we can be lifted up. He came to us so that we would come to Him. He initiates, we respond. The day we gave our life to Christ was a product of His prompting. He invaded our time and space with His love, drawing us to Him.

This pattern never wavers. God is always working on His plan for our lives, and bringing it to completion.

"Therefore you shall be perfect, just as your Father in heaven is perfect."
Jesus Christ

"For I know the thoughts that I think toward you, says the Lord, thoughts of peace and not of evil, to give you a future and a hope," Scripture records in Jeremiah 29:11. Our lives continue to unfold the same way as they did when God saved us: He initiates, and we

respond. God is very serious about initiating, as we can read in Isaiah 55:8–11:

> *"For My thoughts are not your thoughts,*
> *Nor are your ways My ways," says the LORD.*
> *"For as the heavens are higher than the earth,*
> *So are My ways higher than your ways,*
> *And My thoughts than your thoughts.*
>
> *"For as the rain comes down, and the snow from*
> *   heaven,*
> *And do not return there,*
> *But water the earth,*
> *And make it bring forth and bud,*
> *That it may give seed to the sower*
> *And bread to the eater,*
> *So shall My word be that goes forth from My*
> *   mouth;*
> *It shall not return to Me void,*
> *But it shall accomplish what I please,*
> *And it shall prosper in the thing for which*
> *   I sent it."*

The water God gives us is used in many different ways. It grows every part of our lives, bringing forth great fruit and blessing. Eventually, the water returns to heaven through the process of evaporation – continuing a cycle that never ceases. When God speaks a word to us, it changes us: it becomes sustenance for our spirit. Our role is to share that life with others, and to return it to Him through praise and worship. The beauty of walking with God, of being dependent upon Him, is that He gives us exactly what we need to fulfill His commands. Because Christians understand the process of salvation, and that He draws near to us to provoke us to draw near to Him, we can trust that His requests will come with the necessary provision to see them followed up. Whatever God wants from us, He will first give us.

Let God love you! Practice coming to Him. Involve Him in everything you face. Develop conversational prayers as well as crafted prayers. Continually ask for grace and wisdom, then they will not only be present when you need them, but your awareness in the spirit will appropriate them successfully.

Learn to rest in God's word. Meditate (think deeply) on it. Allow your heart (emotions) to connect with what God is saying. Refuse any thought that contradicts the truth. Acknowledge God's Presence with gratitude. Confess to your heart that He is with you ... He is present now. If your emotions cannot detect Him, your faith assuredly will!

> "Your Father knows the things you have need of before you ask Him."
> Jesus Christ

Activate your will, then your mind will change and your emotions must eventually follow suit. Then your soul will submit to your spirit for your benefit and growth.

NB. See journal, *Towards a Powerful Inner Life.*

It takes God to love God: "We love Him because He first loved us." To properly love Him, we must have His love touch down in our hearts. Only then can we return to Him that highest form of love in worship, lifestyle, and prayer. If God is calling us to a higher love for Him, we can rest assured that He has already deposited more of His love into our hearts.

The same principle holds true in prayer. John wrote in 1 John 5:14–15: *"Now this is the confidence that we have in Him, that if we ask anything according to His will, He hears us. And if we know that He hears us, whatever we ask, we know that we have the petitions that we have asked of Him."* Prayer involves finding out what God wants to do and then asking Him to do it. Before we pray, we must listen for the will of God, so we know what we are to pray for. Prayer comes from God: He tells us His will and we agree. His will descends, our prayers ascend.

"Every good gift and every perfect gift is from above, and comes down from the Father of lights, with whom there is no variation or shadow of turning," wrote James in James 1:17. There is no shadow of turning in God: we always know exactly where we stand with Him. He never changes in the middle of a test. *"Of His own will He brought us forth by the word of truth, that we might be a kind of firstfruits of His creatures,"* James continued in verse 18. We are God's gift to Himself. He truly is our source.

God's love

The most important thing in God's heart for us is love.
All blessings flow from that holy, noble, overwhelming
love. In Ephesians 3:14–21, we see how full that love is:

> *For this reason I bow my knees to the Father of our
> Lord Jesus Christ, from whom the whole family in
> heaven and earth is named, that He would grant you,
> according to the riches of His glory, to be
> strengthened with might through His Spirit in the
> inner man, that Christ may dwell in your hearts
> through faith; that you, being rooted and grounded in
> love, may be able to comprehend with all the saints
> what is the width and length and depth and height –
> to know the love of Christ which passes knowledge;
> that you may be filled with all the fullness of God.*
>
> *Now to Him who is able to do exceedingly
> abundantly above all that we ask or think, according
> to the power that works in us, to Him be glory in the
> church by Christ Jesus to all generations, forever
> and ever. Amen.*

To avoid being feeble, ask God for strength. Ask Him
for it, before you need it. Good prayer is always
previous. For example, "Be my strength today Father, in
all that I may face. Grant me that Your strength in me
will enable me to give support to another. Amen."

There is a glorious inner strength that operates in us simply because we are in Christ and He is in us. Trade on that. Reckon on that. Exploit the Presence of Christ in your faith and dependence. God loves that approach. He is here, count on Him. This is the essential nature of fullness ... not being empty-handed in the critical moment.

If our spirituality is going to be meaningful and significant, then we must take time to comprehend the fullness of God's love for us individually. What does it mean for me to be surrounded by God's love? How am I supposed to be overwhelmed by the certainty of it? Who is God's love reaching out to, through me?

We are called to be rooted in God's love, so that we can be filled with "all the fullness of God." This passage is our mission on earth. We need to come to terms with the width and length and height and depth of God's love for us. This love surpasses knowledge. In other words, it is so full and mysterious that it is beyond our human abilities to know.

> "Look at the birds of the air, for they neither sow nor reap nor gather into barns; yet your heavenly Father feeds them. Are you not of more value than they?"
> Jesus Christ

But God, through His glory, changes us to experience it more fully. When we live in the fullness of that love, we give Him glory in return. He gives first, and we return the gift to Him.

The power of the promise of this Scripture is profound. God will do *"exceedingly abundantly"* more than we could ever ask or think. What an extravagant God! The Father is not operating on a tight budget; He is not an economist. He doesn't try to make every penny count. Instead, He lavishes everything because His love is so magnificent.

God's love is broad enough to cover everything, and long enough to last through eternity. It is high enough to reign over heaven, and deep enough to redeem anyone or anything. This is the extravagant love of God which we need to live in.

God's love is enshrined in Jesus' first commandment to us. *"And you shall love the LORD your God with all your heart, with all your soul, with all your mind, and with all your strength,"* Jesus said in Mark 12:30. This is more than a command; it's a promise. We shall love the Lord your God because it is in all of us to want to love Him more. God commands us to love Him because He commands it of Himself. He will not ask us to do something He is not prepared to do first. He loves each of us with all of His heart, all of His soul, all of His mind, and all of His strength. And because He loves us like this, we can love Him in the same way.

intentional love

God has intentionally loved us. There is power in such intentional love. It is the most dynamic, most fulfilling, most releasing, most overcoming, most dominating force in the world. The power of God's love should leave us in a state of shock and awe. How can He be so wonderful? In our sinfulness, corruption, and pettiness, the love of God is splendid. How can we not be filled with awe by it? The love of God has the power to devastate sin.

God's intentional love carries authority, influence, and privilege with it. In it lies God's favor, the open display of God's goodness at all times. We can have complete confidence in the fact that it is the nature of God to be totally and intentionally good to us.

Why doesn't such outrageous love shock more of us? The problem for many is that they find themselves looking at their circumstances rather than the nature of God. God leads us into all things, both good and bad. On the bad days, He wants to be something for us. In those moments, He can banish fear and anxiety. But to do that, we have to be put in a situation where we face fear. If we grab a hold of Him and His love in those terrible moments, He will lift us up to a place in His love where we will never feel that anxiety again.

God allows in His wisdom what He could easily prevent by His power. An immature Christian only wants to be rescued from difficult situations. A more mature individual recognizes the growth opportunity in each circumstance.

We can grow in our peace, joy, faith, confidence, authority, gifting, etc. Ask questions: what is the Father doing? What is this situation for? How will it develop me? Sometimes He wants to eradicate fear by asking us to face it first.

God delivers us from issues not by enabling us, but by dropping us right into it. "I'm right here," He says. "I want you to learn to be with Me so that this thing can never touch you again." In every circumstance, we must stand in the situation and look for God. We know He's there somewhere: we just have to open our eyes to see Him. *"I will never leave you nor forsake you,"* He promised, and we can take Him at His word.

He is our Keeper as well as our Deliverer. Sometimes He sets us free instantly, and at other times our freedom comes through a process. If the Father commits you to a process, He is definitely teaching you about His power to keep you. The key to process is relationship. Keeping and being kept are always about walking in step with the Father in a relational context. Your experience of God will grow outrageously as you follow His routine to keep you.

> "If you have faith as a mustard seed, you will say to this mountain, 'Move from here to there,' and it will move; and nothing will be impossible for you."
> Jesus Christ

NB. See journal, *God's Keeping Power.*

We must look for Him with a sliver of faith. Our emotions are not the key to finding God, our faith is. A tiny bit of faith in a great big God goes a long way. When we have that mustard seed of faith, we have everything we need to find God, because He is never far from us.

We all have enough faith to locate God therefore! Believe He is present in your will and your mind will open up to revelation of what He wishes to accomplish.

God will allow – and sometimes engineer – situations that are designed to establish our child-like simplicity. He wants to renew our minds. In Philippians 4:7, Paul says, *"the peace of God, which surpasses all understanding, will guard your hearts and minds through Christ Jesus."* We can extrapolate from this Scripture that situations that contain opportunities to be anxious are actually a test of our peace.

This principle can be applied to every problem we face. Issues where we feel inadequate or insecure test us in our ability to depend on God. In those situations, we usually fall into the trap of trying to prove ourselves, becoming locked in performance Christianity. And yet the Holy Spirit, in those moments, is trying to establish our dependence on God. Our test is to learn how to translate our insecurity into vulnerability toward God.

Sometimes, we can be in situations that seem overwhelming. The odds are stacked so high against us that the circumstances are virtually insurmountable. But in those moments, the Holy Spirit is working on developing our sense of wonder. We can either be intimidated by life or learn to be fascinated by God. We have that choice.

Human beings are always magnifying their own

issues, seeing things bigger than they really are. And yet, it is God who we need to magnify; we are called to see Him as big as He really is. In the light of His stature, our problems become insignificant. Someone once asked me when the gift of patience comes. "Usually when trouble knocks on the door," I answered. "Patience and trouble always arrive together; we just choose which one we'll let in." Self-control arrives at the same moment as we feel out of control. Joy arrives at the same time as grief. On our journey with God, He has given us many, many, many, many, many provisions. Every problem has a provision attached to it: we just have to see God's love for ourselves.

When we look up and see that God is with us, our face brightens and our steps lighten. "God is with us," we say boldly. "Who can be against us?" The joy of dependency is more than just a mindset; it's a lifestyle. We live dependently, we think dependently, we speak dependently, we see dependently. We become the very people God has called us to be, enjoying His favor and love. We believe in His love to be the provision for every problem.

> "Those who are well have no need of a physician, but those who are sick. But go and learn what this means: 'I desire mercy and not sacrifice.'"
> Jesus Christ

We are not here to doubt – we are here to know. We must pass from faith into knowledge, giving to others everything God has given to us. When we pass into knowledge, we have become what God wants to be for us. The exchange is in full bloom. The very thing that He has been for us, we are now for Him.

being grateful and awestruck

God's blessing should propel us into thanksgiving. Our excitement over what He is doing must manifest itself in gratitude. Thankfulness is something we need to do every day of our lives. Whether life is good or bad, we always have something to give thanks for. Why is this important? Because thanksgiving attracts the Holy Spirit to us.

God will never be anything less than overwhelmingly gracious, merciful, kind, compassionate, good, patient, gentle and faithful to us. God has faith about us and what we can become. He's not embarrassed by our weakness; He trusts us. Believing in these qualities should lead us naturally into gratitude.

> "He to whom this emotion is a stranger, who can no longer pause to wonder and stand rapt in awe, is as good as dead: his eyes are closed."
> Albert Einstein

How big is God to us? Walking with Him isn't about how small we are, but how big He is. Everything the Holy Spirit does should teach us about the sovereignty, supremacy, and majesty of God. Who can not stand and wonder at God's greatness? In our complete weakness, He gives us His strength. He has called each of us to do something that is completely impossible by our own strength. None of us are capable of fulfilling His call or gift – unless we rely totally on Him.

It is vital that we be awestruck by the nature of God. In our worship, we must be astonished and overwhelmed by God's kindness to us. There are certain songs that leave me crying like a two-year-old: they stir my sense of wonder over the beauty of God's character. Psalm 27 does the same thing to me:

> *The LORD is my light and my salvation;*
> *Whom shall I fear?*
> *The LORD is the strength of my life;*
> *Of whom shall I be afraid?*
> *When the wicked came against me*
> *To eat up my flesh,*
> *My enemies and foes,*
> *They stumbled and fell.*
> *Though an army may encamp against me,*
> *My heart shall not fear;*
> *Though war may rise against me,*
> *In this I will be confident.*
>
> *One thing I have desired of the LORD,*
> *That will I seek:*
> *That I may dwell in the house of the LORD*
> *All the days of my life,*
> *To behold the beauty of the LORD,*
> *And to inquire in His temple.*
> *For in the time of trouble*

He shall hide me in His pavilion;
In the secret place of His tabernacle
He shall hide me;
He shall set me high upon a rock.

And now my head shall be lifted up above my
*   enemies all around me;*
Therefore I will offer sacrifices of joy in His
*   tabernacle;*
I will sing, yes, I will sing praises to the LORD.

The imagery and wonder in those verses inspire me. David's absolute faith in God astonishes me – he never wavers when it comes to God's character. I can sense David's awe of God. *"One thing I have desired of the LORD, that will I seek: that I may dwell in the house of the LORD all the days of my life, to behold the beauty of the LORD, and to inquire in His temple."* What a stunning line!

It should be impossible for us to ever tire of thanking and praising God. Like the old hymn by Frederick Lehman, "The Love of God," states:

The love of God is greater far
Than tongue or pen could ever tell
It goes beyond the highest star
And reaches to the lowest hell
The guilty pair bowed down with care
God gave His Son to win
His erring child He reconciled
And pardoned from his sin

O love of God, how rich and pure
How measureless and strong
It shall forevermore endure
The saints' and angels' song.

Could we with ink the ocean fill
And were the skies of parchment made
Were every stock on earth a quill
And every man a scribe by trade
To write the love of God above
Would drain the ocean dry
Nor could the scroll contain the whole
Though stretched from sky to sky

God the Father

Enjoying God depends, in no small measure, on our ability to be present in our circumstances. Can we look to Him throughout the day? Can we trust Him with everything all the time? These are the questions which we must wrestle with.

Sometimes life threatens to overwhelm us, and we find it difficult to deal with issues. We often need revelation to know what is in God's heart for us in that particular time. Wisdom is the understanding about how God thinks and how He likes to work and the ability to position yourself accordingly.

Revelation is hidden from casual perception. Read 1 Corinthians 2:6–13 to see how normally we only access the hidden wisdom when we hide in God's heart ourselves. We must learn the art of abiding; to stay, dwell and remain in God. At the first hint of trouble, to turn and burrow deeper into His nature. To hide in God is our grace and our salvation. To dwell in who He is for us.

When we firstly hide in Him, we become conscious of Who He is in Himself. Eventually His life and our confidence surges up through our spirit and we have the courage to stand in the place of grace that Father has picked out for us. Abiding in Christ enables me to find solace and rest; just to be.

This is a major part of our inheritance in relationship with God. It is so important, it was a critical part of both Old and New Covenants ... John 15 in the New Testament, and the following passage from David's journal, Psalm 27:4–6:

> *One thing I have desired of the LORD,*
> *That will I seek:*
> *That I may dwell in the house of the LORD*
> *All the days of my life,*
> *To behold the beauty of the LORD,*
> *And to inquire of His temple.*
> *For in the time of trouble*
> *He shall hide me in His pavilion;*
> *In the secret place of His tabernacle*
> *He shall hide me;*
> *He shall set me high upon a rock.*

And now my head shall be lifted up above my
enemies all around me;
Therefore I will offer sacrifices of joy in His
tabernacle;
I will sing, yes, I will sing praises to the LORD.

God Himself is the perfect hideaway. In that secret place we receive the hidden wisdom of how to conduct ourselves. We learn how to stand, wait and see the salvation of God. We develop our attitude of faith, our internal approach to the Father.

I believe that it is our spiritual attitude that determines what we will experience in the Spirit every day. If we come into a day glum, defeated, and bitter, we will have experiences to reflect those feelings. But if we enter a new day with the awe of God in our hearts, our lives will be glorious.

One thing I know, as the father of three children, is that all kids want to be confident about their parents. My goal, as a dad, is to show my children that God is a million times better than I. He is more generous and extravagant than any of us can imagine. I want to model to them the Father heart of God, because what we think about God is the single most important thing in our lives.

God is more concerned with what comes out of us than what comes against us. He wants to use every situation in life to teach us more about Himself. As His children, we can look beyond our circumstances and claim the blessing that is always present in moments like that. As Paul wrote in Ephesians 5:8–10: *"For you were once darkness, but now you are light in the Lord. Walk as children of light (for the fruit of the Spirit is in all goodness, righteousness, and truth), finding out what is acceptable to the Lord."*

> "Worry never robs tomorrow of its sorrow, it only saps today of its joy."
> Leo Buscaglia

We lose our innocence when we protect ourselves from harm because we form a barrier that actually keeps God on the outside. It is easier to be open and become wounded than to protect ourselves and become hard. Why? Because it is easier to get healed than to have to break down the barrier that we erect to protect ourselves.

I would rather be innocent and get killed than be suspicious, cynical, mistrustful, or negative. I think it's better for God to resurrect me than to put up barriers to keep Him out. Becoming children of light means that we are open to God's nature and we trust Him to do what He says He is going to do. We learn how to bow down to His goodness and kindness. Such confidence changes our lifestyle from one of self-preservation to incredible grace. Being children of light changes the way we show up in the world.

Innocence takes vulnerability – being humble and transparent about our weaknesses. In my home church in Southampton, England, we have a rule for anyone speaking in a meeting: the speaker must tell at least one story against themselves. We must have full disclosure and humility. And we listen for that story. We don't want pretense in our pulpit.

Child-like Christians allow God to peel off what is false and destructive in our thinking. What others think about us doesn't matter: it's what we fail to appreciate about the goodness of God that harms us. Our lack of awe is our own doing. If we don't feel right about the majesty and sovereignty of God, than I don't see how we can feel right about ourselves. The grace of God helps us to feel good about our lives. I know the things God wants to change in me and I look forward to them. But I still feel good about who He has made me to be so far. The more we are cut off from our true center in Christ, the more destructive our behavior towards others can become.

God's purity is His protection for us. Look at this passage from Romans 12:

> *Repay no one evil for evil. Have regard for good things in the sight of all men. If it is possible, as much as depends on you, live peaceably with all men. Beloved, do not avenge yourselves, but rather give place to wrath; for it is written, "Vengeance is Mine, I will repay," says the Lord. Therefore "If your enemy is hungry, feed him; if he is thirsty, give him a drink; for in so doing you will heap coals of fire on his head." Do not be overcome by evil, but overcome evil with good.*

We must learn how to have a pure response when trouble arises. Because God is pure, we can purify our actions and heart with the hope and the help of the Holy Spirit. Can we see the beauty of the other person, or only the ugliness of his carnality? Will we show the other person the beauty God has put in us, or only our own sinfulness?

Hypocrisy sneaks up on us, whenever we think we are better than someone else. In Matthew 7:1–5 Jesus spoke movingly about our own perspective leading us not only into becoming a cynic, but also lacking in vision.

Whenever we take an issue up with someone else, we must ensure that our prejudice is not showing. The "speck and log" scenario affect us more than we think. Sometimes our self-righteousness prevents us seeing the good, however small, in others. We see this in the fundamentalist evangelical community where Christians cannot see the good in any pre-Christian. Goodness does not start the moment we confess Christ, it is at work in us long before we submit to His Lordship.

There is treasure in every earthen vessel. The Gospel brings that treasure to the light and gives it a name. Jesus saw Nathaniel under a tree and commented enthusiastically about an aspect of his character. John 1:45–51 records: *"... A man in whom there is no guile! ... "* That opening remark led to a very prophetic conversation that was full of promise. Nathaniel's response to Jesus was to see Him as He really was, and to confess the Son of God as Lord.

It never hurts to do good and speak well to others, no matter who they are or what type of background they have. Sometimes the log in our own eye is just that we have an over-inflated sense of our own importance. We don't see others, except in a small way. People feel overlooked and unimportant.

If you have a desire to correct what you see in someone else, take a quick eye test first. How many people do you pass by, because you fail to see who they are? What about people around you whom you see regularly but with whom you only exchange the odd pleasantry? How many lonely people live their lives in quiet desperation because nobody sees them?

> "All of the animals, except man, know that the principal business of life is to enjoy it."
> Anonymous

Whatever blocks our vision will cause us to miss God. We will miss Him in terms of His Presence. We will miss seeing Him in opportunities that He both allows and creates. Above all, we will miss seeing Him in the people around us, and we will be the poorer because of it.

turning away to draw someone near

Maintaining a sense of wonder takes dedication and hard work, especially in the face of conflict. Can we remain unsuspecting? Are we prepared to give an answer for our faith but, at the same time, not have our mind so settled that we defend our position to the death? The moment we enter a situation with our armor on, we put a wall between us and the other person. We can't listen; we can only defend.

The armor of God is against our enemy, not people. Goodness and kindness always prevail. Goodness overcomes evil; kindness leads to repentance. Humility gives us soft eyes and a soft voice in time of opposition or conflict. Gentleness disarms people. All the fruit of the Spirit are brilliant for using in situations of relational misunderstanding or difficulty. Patience enables us to hang in there, quietly believing the best. Faithfulness enables us to endure and stay true to the heart of God and our own inner values of the Holy Spirit. Self-control prevents our carnality from revealing itself. Peace stops us from reacting angrily. Love enables us to reach out with a blessing, because real love always has a gift to bestow. Joy enables us to smile and laugh at ourselves. Happiness is contagious.

There are times, however, when we have to turn away from people – but we can only turn away from them when we have an agenda to see them restored. In Romans 16:17–20, the Apostle Paul offered this advice to churches dealing with dissension:

Now I urge you, brethren, note those who cause divisions and offenses, contrary to the doctrine which you learned, and avoid them. For those who are such do not serve our Lord Jesus Christ, but their own belly, and by smooth words and flattering speech deceive the hearts of the simple. For your obedience has become known to all. Therefore I am glad on your behalf; but I want you to be wise in what is good, and simple concerning evil. And the God of peace will crush Satan under your feet shortly.

Again, the only reason we turn away from people is to see them restored. It sounds a little bit like Orwellian doublespeak, but it is absolutely true. Once, while leading a church, I put my best friend out of fellowship. He was one of the people I loved most in the world, but I had to put him out because he was being willfully disobedient, rebellious, treacherous, and divisive. He was manipulating camps of people into going to war against one another. It was awful. He had a bee in his bonnet about something and wouldn't – or couldn't – let it go.

I loved him so much that I tried everything to keep him. I went further with him than I would have with a lot of people, to my shame. But he would not budge on the issue so, finally, I had to say, "My friend, I need to put you out of fellowship."

"What?" he replied, nonplussed. "You and I have been friends for years!"

"Yes," I said, "but I'm friends with God as well, and you're not right now. You prove it every time you open your mouth. You have disrupted our church and set people against one another. All of this bitterness is coming out of your heart. We've tried for weeks and weeks to get you to see what you're doing, but you refuse to see what the Holy Spirit is saying to you. I'm convinced that you'll never see it if you stay here, but by putting you out there, you just might."

My friend never believed I'd do it, but I did. On the next Sunday morning, I stood at the church's front door and said, "You're not coming in, pal." It broke my heart; I cried and cried as I turned him away.

Four weeks later, he was back in church. As soon as he saw I was serious, he went away and thought about what he was doing and the pain he was causing me. What else could he do but seek the Lord? The deception, or whatever it was, lifted off of him. When we first sat down to talk about it, he told me that as soon I had put him out, he began to plot his way back in. "But the only way back in was to repent," he said. When he asked me if he could return, I told him "no."

> "Life is to be fortified by many friendships. To love and to be loved is the greatest happiness of existence."
> Sydney Smith

"What do I have to do?" he asked.

"You know what you have to do," I said. "You said all kinds of things privately that you need to put right publicly. If you come back, you're going to have to apologize to the whole church for what you've done. Don't spare yourself: you need to humble yourself." It was one of the hardest things I've ever done, but he did exactly what he had to, and we're good friends today.

I had to remain innocent even while dealing with the divisiveness of my best friend. It's a difficult paradox to remain unsuspecting but have our senses trained to discern good and evil. *"But solid food belongs to those who are of full age, that is, those who by reason of use have their senses exercised to discern both good and evil,"* says Hebrews 5:14. We can be unsuspecting and wise at the same time, asking God some important questions. Is this You, God? If it's not You, is it the enemy? And if it isn't the enemy, is it just the spirit of man? The gift of discerning spirits enables us to be wise in knowing what is good.

Christ the priest

When do we need a friend the most? When we fall down, of course. When we've done something monumentally stupid. We don't need friends who will be embarrassed by our shortcomings, but ones who will help cover what we're not. I love that my friends will defend me to the death but, at the same time, won't let me get away with anything. Nowhere is this principle more evident than in our friendship with Jesus, as Hebrews 4:12–16 explains:

> *For the word of God is living and powerful, and sharper than any two-edged sword, piercing even to*

the division of soul and spirit, and of joints and marrow, and is a discerner of the thoughts and intents of the heart. And there is no creature hidden from His sight, but all things are naked and open to the eyes of Him to whom we must give account.

Seeing then that we have a great High Priest who has passed through the heavens, Jesus the Son of God, let us hold fast our confession. For we do not have a High Priest who cannot sympathize with our weaknesses, but was in all points tempted as we are, yet without sin. Let us therefore come boldly to the throne of grace, that we may obtain mercy and find grace to help in time of need.

The priesthood of Christ gives us continuous access to the presence of God. What a great thought! God understands us. He knows our weaknesses. He's never disillusioned with us. And, in that need, we have confident access to the throne of God's grace. God's throne – His seat of power – is also His seat of generosity and grace. We receive His mercy when we most need it. The test for us is to extend that same mercy to those who come to us. They get the same treatment from God – shouldn't they get the same treatment from us?

"The most wonderful of all things in life, I believe, is the discovery of another human being with whom one's relationship has a glowing depth, beauty, and joy as the years increase. This inner progressiveness of love between two human beings is a most marvelous thing, it cannot be found by looking for it or by passionately wishing for it. It is a sort of Divine accident."
Hugh Walpole, Sr.

We can know, with confidence, what God wants to do in every situation. Prayer is simply finding out what God wants to do and then asking Him to do it. I believe that we need to listen to Him before we pray – not after! Sadly, we have been taught or trained to jump right in and pray away. But God wants us to seek His solution, not our own.

Having a healthy sense of wonder about who God is leads us into thanksgiving, which opens the door to His presence for us. By thanking Him for what He is trying to do in us in the situation, we open our ears and calm our soul to hear Him more clearly. "What is it you want me to pray?" we can ask God calmly. Instead of praying out of our panic or fear, we can pray out of our child-likeness. "I believe God will accomplish what He wants to accomplish," we can say. We can have faith that if we ask anything according to His will, He hears us. There is no ambiguity in this at all: just simple confidence.

the thrill of victory

Being joyful shouldn't be difficult when we know that our Father has already secured the victory in everything. By shifting our paradigm to believe that every challenge and issue is merely another opportunity for God to be Himself, we can share the thrill of His victory. We can be gleeful about God. Children are always gleeful when they know they are receiving a gift, or about to win at something. We can have that same delight, that same carefree excitement, in God. *"My yoke is easy and My burden is light,"* Jesus said in Matthew 11:30. Almost since the moment He said that, Christians have been trying to make their burdens heavy and hard. But God is actually very easy to be with.

"Every good gift and every perfect gift is from above, and comes down from the Father of lights, with whom there is no variation or shadow of turning," the Apostle James wrote in James 1:17. God cannot turn on us; He will not abandon us. He is for us – and every gift in our lives comes from His hand. God is completely consistent. This faithfulness can act as the bedrock of our relationship with Him: we know He

> "I am mentally preparing myself for the five-year-old mind. I want to come down to their physical limitations and up to their sense of wonder and awe.
> Shinichi Suzuki

was fully there, *is* fully there, and always *will be* fully there for us. How can our hearts not sing for joy at such a thought?

Christians are God's visual aids for the earth. He uses us to show the world what heaven will be like. How many people, right now, have the wrong impression that heaven will be a place of dull hymns, old-fashioned music, and a glum God? Where do you think this idea comes from? It flows out of the world's dislike for dull, old-fashioned, glum Christians! *"Of His own will He brought us forth by the word of truth, that we might be a kind of firstfruits of His creatures,"* James added

(James 1:18). We are the first crop of God's provision that the world sees.

dullness and astonishment

We are caught up in a war between dullness and astonishment. Jesus recognized that the heart of people had become dull. They could not see, nor hear, nor understand. Matthew records how their ability to perceive what God was really like caused them to live below the place of acceptable revelation (Matthew 13:10-17).

They had a superficial surface relationship with the Father, and also with other believers. The Pharisees, in particular, completely failed to recognize Jesus as the Messiah. They had studied for years about this visitation of God. They knew everything there was to know ... but dullness prevented them from seeing.

After all the miracles and adventures in the book of Acts, Paul's final parting words to that generation were about dullness (Acts 28:25-29). Dullness is our inability to see God as He really is! Jesus put a child in the midst of His disciples and said in Matthew 18:3: *"Unless you are converted **and** become as little children, you will by no means enter the kingdom of heaven."* Children perceive on a different level than adults. Far more trusting, children are open to mystery; they live, wide-eyed with astonishment.

Unless we recapture a child-like approach to the Father, we cannot enter into a real experience of kingdom life. The kingdom is only open and available to those who have a capacity for astonishment. People who love simplicity, believe outrageously.

There are dozens and dozens of scriptures that portray a people who are amazed, astonished and who marvel at the wonderful ways of God and His wondrous works that are simply marvelous! It's hard to talk honestly about God without using superlatives ... amazing, astonishing, marvelous, wonderful, wondrous!

Jesus was not God pretending to be a man. He really was a man. The apostle Peter said this:

> *Jesus of Nazareth, a Man attested by God to you by miracles, wonders and signs which God did through Him in your midst, as you yourselves also know.*
>
> (Acts 2:22)

Jesus could not heal the sick, cast out demons, or raise the dead on His own. He says in John 5:19–20:

> *Most assuredly, I say to you, the Son can do nothing of Himself, but what He sees the Father do; for whatever He does, the Son also does in like manner. For the Father loves the Son, and shows Him all things that He Himself does; and He will show Him greater works than these, **that you may marvel.***

Jesus repeatedly said that He could do nothing of Himself and that He only said and did what the Father was saying and doing (John 5:30; 6:38; 8:28; 12:49; 14:10). He wasn't being humble, He was being truthful.

He chose to live a limited lifestyle. As the second Adam He wanted to live with the same conditions that redeemed man would have to contend with in walking with the Father. He purposefully came to model what a man in right relationship with God could do in the natural realm. When He came down from heaven, He brought His world with Him. He came with a greater reality. It was the reality of what a right relationship with God can achieve.

If He did signs and wonders as God, then these cannot be possible for us. But if He did them as a Man, in right relationship with the Father, then everything is possible for us in the Spirit.

This is what John records in 5:20 that we are supposed to marvel at ... our redemption in Christ makes all things attainable. The norm of spirituality is that we live in a place of wide-eyed astonishment, permanently excited, constantly amazed!

Jesus healed a demoniac who was blind and deaf; Matthew 12:23 records that everyone was amazed. Luke records in 4:36 how an unclean spirit was rebuked and a man healed, which provoked astonishment. The disciples saw Jesus walking on water in a storm and Mark records in 6:51, *"They were greatly amazed in themselves beyond measure and marveled."*

Everywhere Jesus went people were dumbfounded with astonishment; they were ecstatic that heaven had come to earth in an ordinary man in right relationship with God (is not this Joseph the Carpenter's son?).

Everyone knew the paralyzed guy. Four friends made sure he got in front of Jesus. His healing caused amazement; people were glorifying God and Luke 5:26 records they were filled with fear, saying, *"We have seen strange things today!"* Amazement, glory and fear (reverent awe) ... astonishing! Luke states in 9:43 that wherever Jesus went people were all amazed at the majesty of God and marveled at all Jesus did.

We begin to see the same response to the disciples at Pentecost. Acts 2:7–10 records how these ordinary guys spoke in languages they had never learned, causing all who heard to be amazed and marvel; Acts 3:10–12 records how people were filled with wonder and amazement when Peter healed the man at the gate. People came together out of sheer astonishment to hear Peter who made it clear that he had no personal power to heal.

It was not just miracles that were amazing. Acts 9:21 records how people were astonished at Paul's revelatory gifting, just as they had been with the young Jesus as recorded by Luke in 2:41–50.

Jesus continually taught as one having authority,

which was astonishing given His working background. Matthew records in 13:53–58 how people were astonished in Jesus' own synagogue, *"Where did this Man get this wisdom and these mighty works?"* (verse 54). They knew His family and background, so their astonishment soon turned to being offended at Him.

No-one could be neutral around Jesus! He raised a girl from the dead and Mark 5:42 records that everyone was overcome with amazement. Luke 7:31–37 details Jesus putting His fingers in a deaf man's hears, spitting and touching the man's tongue and his ears opened and he could speak properly, and that people were astonished beyond measure, astonished with a great astonishment.

Mark's gospel records in chapter 10 how the revelatory wisdom of Jesus opened up His disciples to truth in a way that caused astonishment, and in Mark 11:18 how the scribes and chief priests feared His revelation because all the people were amazed by it.

Jesus entered Peter's fishing world with no experience of the craft, but Luke records in 5:3–11 that Jesus caused utter amazement and astonishment at what He did next. God's capacity to sneak up on us and bring surprise and astonishment to us is overwhelming on days. Acts 10:44–45 records how Peter, still a little nervous about being in a Gentile house, is delicately explaining the gospel when the Holy Spirit fell on people suddenly, in mid sermon. This time it was the apostolic team who were astonished! Peter was given a "get out of jail free" card by an angel (Acts 12:16); that was pretty astonishing!

Astonishment follows true spirituality. This sense of wonder was apparent in the Old Covenant also. David was a man after God's heart, because he lived with wonder. His journal, the Psalms, was full of references to a state of mind and heart that remained with him on the hazardous journey of his life.

> *Many, O LORD My God, are your wonderful works*
> *... Your thoughts toward us*
> *Cannot be ... numbered.* (Psalm 40:5)

For David, everything about God was marvelous, too high, wondrous, amazing, phenomenal, sensational. He would talk about God in superlatives, ensuring generations were kept informed of God's greatness, as in Psalm 78:4. Repeatedly he would use this phrase, no doubt written on his own heart, that is found in Psalm 107:8: *"Oh, that men would give thanks to the LORD for His goodness, and for His wonderful works to the children of men!"* Psalm 119:129 is an example of how God's testimonies filled David with wonder.

David's understanding of God caused him to live in wonder and amazement. On days it seemed like everything was too brilliant, too incredible, as he writes in Psalm 139:6. Having wonder and living in wonder will change our whole persona. It is a high place in which to abide; to be so astonished at God that everything becomes possible. His world has entered ours, and we are open-mouthed at His glory, amazed by His heart for us, astonished that all the constraints must disappear to a man or woman who is prepared to live in child-like simplicity and wonder.

One moment Isaiah is mulling over the fact that his conversations are not clean, and the next he writes in chapter 6 of how he is entering into a conversation in heaven. An angel touches his lips with a live coal as he stands astonished at the sight of God and angels, his ears filled with the sound of wings, voices and doors shaking. God, it seems, has different ways of introducing us to awe, wonder and astonishment.

Small wonder, then, that Isaiah writes in 25:1 and 28:29 of how he had a perspective on God that gripped his heart. All the prophets had that same sense of wonder and astonishment. Part of Jeremiah's life message was enshrined in this word:

"But let him who glories glory in this,
That he understands and knows Me,
That I am the LORD, exercising lovingkindness,
*   judgment, and righteousness in the earth.*
For in these I delight," says the LORD.

(Jeremiah 9:24)

Joel's message in 2:25–26 was:

> ... *I will restore you* ...
> *You shall eat in plenty and be satisfied,*
> *And praise the name of the LORD your God,*
> *Who has dealt wondrously with you;*
> *And My people shall never be put to shame.*

What is our modern-day shame as believers? It is that we have denied the Lord the right and the opportunity to be wonderful. We have watered down the power of the gospel, displaced the Holy Spirit and reduced the glory of the Body of Christ to a bunch of impotent people who have a form of godliness but deny the power. We have formed a theology around our impotence that keeps us earthbound and moribund. (Look up that last word in the dictionary, then get as far away from it as you can and you'll start living in wonder!) Pharisees always want to pour the cold water of common sense onto a spirit of revelation.

We have lost our ability to be simple and astonished. The biggest enemy in the Church is the one that we don't see. In many churches our doctrine has deceived us about the intentions and the ability of the Father. To actually believe that God has power, but chose only to use it for a brief time in the Church's history, is a heresy that can only empower the devil.

The Good News is that salvation saves the whole man;

body, soul and spirit. The Good News is health and wholeness personified in Jesus. The Good News is that it shall be on earth as it is in heaven. The Good News is Jesus' words in John 14:12: *"greater works than these he* [who believes in Me] *will do, because I go to My Father."*

Our problem is that the Good News has become OK news. As a result, Christianity is no longer life-changing, but merely life-enhancing. People don't give permission for Jesus to change them into radicals anymore, just into "nice people". The church has become dull, predictable and monotonous.

It was the un-nice brand of spirituality that turned the world upside down. The early disciples were an anti-institutional, category-smashing, evil-threatening ministry, considered to be so dangerous they would have to be killed. Dangerous Christians have ruined lives and captivated hearts. They can no longer abide mediocrity, they are pursuing a spirit of excellence in Christ.

Dullness is the absence of brightness in our souls, where people have lost their sparkle and their joy. In that context, spirituality becomes a duty, not a desire. When we fail to be possessed by God, we forfeit the capacity to dream. Sin is not just about immorality and selfishness. It is living drab, colorless, dreary, stale, unimaginative lives. The greatest enemy of Christianity may well be people who say they believe in Jesus but who are no longer astonished or amazed by Him. We are drowning in dullness.

God's love for us is brilliant. Paul was joyful all the time because he had confidence in God's protection over Him. He wrote in Romans 8:37 – 39: *"We are more than conquerors through Him who loved us. For I am persuaded that neither death nor life, nor angels nor principalities nor powers, nor things present nor things to come, nor height nor depth, nor any other created thing, shall be able to separate us from the love of God which is in Christ Jesus our Lord."* Our task is to enjoy being God's children; to view Him with an innate sense of wonder. *"We are more than conquerors,"* thanks to His love for us – we are condemned to a glorious victory!

Victory is inescapable. We cannot screw it up for God. We cannot avoid His victory. In every issue, circumstance, conflict, disagreement, and attack, God has already won. He can do something in any moment, and our joy is to find out what. People with a child-like faith know this; the idea that it might not work out never even enters their head. It may take time, they think, but God is in control. *"And we know that all things work together for good to those who love God, to those who are the called according to His purpose,"* Paul explained in Romans 8:28.

> "I admire the serene assurance of those who have religious faith. It is wonderful to observe the calm confidence of a Christian with four aces."
> Mark Twain

Every battle is different, and God may have a separate lesson in each. One conflict may teach us about authority, and the next, obedience. A third battle may teach us about submission, and a fourth patience. God wants to show us more and more of His character and nature every day, so He allows opportunities for us to rely on Him. By standing with Him, we can add substance to our faith. Our role in every fight is to ask Him what He wants to teach us, and to co-operate with Him to that end.

While God constantly operates in the fruit of the Spirit, the enemy has no access to it. Satan and the kingdom of darkness cannot be patient. During one of my visits to Africa, I was privileged to go into the jungle with an expert tracker named Mugumbe. We were out there for three days, with just a bedroll, canteen, my knife, and Mugumbe's short, Zulu hunting spear, an assegai.

On the third day, we passed a thicket of thorns and I noticed Mugumbe smile and step out into a small clearing. "Come," he said to me. I looked over his shoulder and saw a pride of seventeen lions.

"Come," Mugumbe said to me.

"Not on your life!" I answered.

"It's okay," he said, "they've all been fed. Come." What choice did I have? The plane was in that direction and Mugumbe was my only hope of finding it. So I stepped out. The instant I did, the lioness stood up and wandered in our direction.

"Look at her belly," Mugumbe said. Her stomach was full, even to my untrained eye.

"Is she pregnant?" I asked.

"No," he replied. "She's already eaten. She's full of meat and won't be able to run."

My carnality showed itself briefly. All I have to do is fun faster than this old fellow, I thought. Then I noticed that he was wearing trainers whilst I had heavy boots. Peace and faith suddenly seemed to be the brighter option!

Mugumbe looked at the lioness and yelled. "Ho! Go back!" And she did! Later, we talked about the experience. "Lions have no patience," he told me. "They only want a quick kill. He doesn't have the physique for a long chase; they're not like cheetahs or leopards. He can only be explosive over a short patch of ground. Anything longer, and it becomes physically impossible for the lion to run."

> "The happiness of the bee and the dolphin is to exist. For man it is to know that and to wonder at it."
> Jacques-Yves Cousteau

Just like those lions, the enemy has no access to the spiritual fruit of patience. If something doesn't develop the way Satan wants, he pulls the plug on the operation. All a Christian has to do is stand with Jesus. The enemy can't fight that! Christ knows how to endure and how to be patient. We can learn those same traits.

a victorious effort

Victory does take effort on our part – but the effort is always well worth it. In my home city of Manchester,

England, a group of churches got together and envisioned a long-term plan for their city. To get the ball rolling, they decided to start saving some money. It took them a few years, but finally they had enough money in the bank to put their plan in motion.

Together, the churches approached Manchester's civic government, police department, social services, and industries with an idea called Eden 2000. With the help of the city's experts, they picked the worst neighborhood in Manchester. This particular subdivision was overridden with crime, its streets were filthy. People lived in bread lines: it had been compared by the media to a war zone. It was a godless, hopeless place.

The churches were undaunted by the challenge. Together, they mobilized 20,000 Christians for a two-week period. These Christians went into the neighborhood and started working. They painted every house; they cleaned up every garden. They picked up trash; they planted roses; they built playgrounds. They prayed for everyone they met. They started two churches. They worked and worked and worked.

In those two weeks, not a single crime was committed in the area. The place, which had once had a crime rate way above the national average, was crime-free. At the end of the two weeks, people were weeping. "Don't leave us!" they said. The neighborhood has been a changed place ever since.

> "Love one another and you will be happy. It's as simple and as difficult as that."
> Michael Leunig

The role of the Church is to make goodness fashionable. There are things that only we can do, because we have the Spirit of God with us. The favor of God was on those Manchester Christians, and the local government is now asking, "Where are you going to hit next?" The goodness shown by these Christians inspired the world. Businesses began donating tools and plants and anything else that was needed. The police donated their time to help. In fact, the police have donated a million pounds for a youth center to be built in another part of town – and they want the Manchester churches to put a youth church in it. These people have seen the fruit of God's love – and they want to help it spread.

Our purpose in life is to bless other people, as Peter writes in 1 Peter 3:9. If we don't release those blessings, we are partially responsible for the sad state of the society we live in. If we have the cure – God's love – and refuse to give it away, we have helped the sickness. Evil is overcome with good. Darkness is shattered by light.

The innocent are not afraid of intimidation. If we have a sense of wonder, we cannot be troubled. Our fear falls away in the light of our fascination with who God is. Will we sanctify Christ in our heart? Will we step back into a place of innocence and purity? Will our sense of wonder be born again? *"If you can believe, all things are possible to him who believes,"* Jesus said in Mark 9:23. *"With men it is impossible, but not with God; for with God all things are possible,"* He added in Mark 10:27.

We can speak with a gentleness and reverence which allows the innocence within to emerge with the Holy Spirit. We can keep a clear conscience. I believe that a rediscovered innocence is much stronger than the original, because we have made the choice in the face of bitter experience. We know what was lost and we never want to lose it again. Christianity is delightfully simple – it's about remaining in Christ and allowing the Holy Spirit to express the intentions of God to somebody else. We each meet hundreds and hundreds of people who have a distorted image of who God is, but our presence can lead them to see Him in a new way.

> "Happiness is inward, and not outward; and so, it does not depend on what we have, but on what we are."
> Henry Van Dyke

Goodness has a power that hell cannot break. Evil is always overcome by good – even a little good. It's like Manchester, a large industrial city. They took 20,000 people into a neighborhood. It was a microcosm of the city, but the shock waves have been enormous. Eden 2000 was featured in local, regional, and national news for two weeks. Every day, the newspapers had updates, interviews, photos, and stories on what was going on. Even now, years later, people still talk about it. They are planning their next hit and the whole city is waiting. Analysts on television still talk about how that neighborhood changed. Good news remains!

loving God

King David is a perfect example of a man who knew how to respond to God's initiative. The prophet Samuel described him best in 1 Samuel 13:14 – *"The Lord has sought for Himself a man after His own heart."* David loved God with all of his heart, mind, soul, and strength. He responded fully to the love God was lavishing on him. This was so remarkable that Paul mentioned it hundreds of years later in Acts 13:22 – *"He raised up for them David as king, to whom also He gave testimony and said, 'I have found David the son of Jesse, a man after My own heart, who will do all My will.'"* Daniel was similarly marked by God. The Lord Himself called Daniel a *"man greatly beloved"* in Daniel 10:11.

Were David and Daniel perfect? No. They still sinned like you and I, and yet they were men after God's own heart. Jesus, on the other hand, was perfect: He was the living embodiment of the fullness of God. But even He only did what He saw the Father doing. God initiated, Jesus responded.

God loves us with all of His soul. Isaiah 53:10 tells us that Jesus' soul was an offering for our sin. God separated Himself from Christ in those dark moments on the Cross so that nothing would ever separate us from Him again.

God loves us with all of His mind, as we know from Jeremiah 29:11. God has thoughts and plans for us that are too good to be imagined. David explained this love in a different way in his psalms. *"Many, O LORD my God, are Your wonderful works which You have done; and Your thoughts toward us cannot be recounted to You in order; if I would declare and speak of them, they are more than can be numbered,"* he sang in Psalm 40:5. *"How precious also are Your thoughts to me, O God! How great is the sum of them! If I should count them, they would be more in number than the sand; when I awake, I am still with You,"* he added in Psalm 139:17–18. David had experiences with God where he felt loved in his own thought life. He understood the thoughts God had toward him, and this gave him such security that even his own thought life reflected that love.

The mind is a powerful tool, and renewing it leads to transformation. *"And do not be conformed to this world, but be transformed by the renewing of your mind, that you may prove what is that good and acceptable and perfect will of God,"* Paul says in Romans 12:2. *"Be renewed in the spirit of your mind, and that you put on the new man which was created according to God, in true righteousness and holiness,"* he added in Ephesians 4:23–24.

The way we think has to be an act of worship. Our minds are the most important place to receive the love of God because what we think about Him is absolutely vital. If we think correctly about God, we will think correctly about ourselves. What we think about God touches our own self. We cannot go through life running ourselves down and trying to magnify God. It doesn't work. *"For I say, through the grace given to me, to everyone who is among you, not to think of himself more highly than he ought to think, but to think soberly, as God has dealt to each one a measure of faith,"* Paul counseled in Romans 12:3. If I may paraphrase: we must think highly of ourselves, but not get stupid about it.

Humility is not about running ourselves down, but about receiving all the fullness that God has while knowing in our heart of hearts that we don't deserve it. True humility results in gratitude and worship. God's thoughts toward us are precious and full of love. *"Beloved, if our heart does not condemn us, we have confidence toward God,"* says 1 John 3:21. Condemnation is not allowed: it is our enemy.

> "Therefore whoever humbles himself as this little child is the greatest in the kingdom of heaven."
> Jesus Christ

Guilt, however, can be our ally. Guilt can be helpful because the whole point of it is to bring us back to the Cross and the forgiveness that resides there. It brings us to a point where we can recognize our need to depend on the mercy of God. Condemnation chases us away from God, but guilt can bring us closer. Part of the Holy Spirit's role is to convict us when we are bad. His conviction pushes us into the presence of God and moves us to kneel and ask for forgiveness. The line between the two is clear: guilt brings us to God, but condemnation drives us away by making us feel completely worthless.

When God convicts us of sin, He also holds out the promise of change. He hands us the one thing that will cancel our sinfulness. In a conference prayer line, I saw lust all over the guy in front of me. He did not need me to tell him about his sin. The Holy Spirit convicts. Our job is to know the gift that comes with conviction.

Looking at him I said, "There is suspended over your life such a weight of purity and holiness that as you enter in to it. you will be changed into another man. All that has held you back from experiencing the fullness of Christ will disappear as you allow the Holy Spirit to establish righteousness. God will help you. He will help you. He will help you! You are His beloved son and I break the power of uncleanness in Jesus' Name. I declare to you that you will be a righteous man."

He wept with relief and gratitude toward God. Promise is the ally of conviction. Together they release healing and wholeness. God always makes us feel valuable in Christ.

"In this is love, not that we loved God, but that He loved us and sent His Son to be the propitiation for our sins," says 1 John 4:10. Propitiation is a big word, but its meaning is powerful: it is what happens when someone wins us back to a place of absolute divine favor by becoming the very thing that robbed us of that favor

in the first place. Sin knocked us out of favor, but Christ's death brought us back.

Favor from God is not an optional extra: it is a necessity. All we can do is grow in that favor. If God is who He says He is, then He deserves a people who live in absolute favor no matter what the circumstance. Christians have nothing to fear. When there is war or rumors of war, we are called to be a company of people who are unafraid. When everyone starts hoarding their money because the stock markets are crashing and the pension funds are failing, we are to be a company of people who give things away. Wouldn't the world be intrigued by a group of people who did everything wrong by their standards and yet succeeded like mad? It's almost like Moses and the Burning Bush: it burned and burned but was never consumed. All it did was draw Moses near.

God deserves such a company of people. He deserves a people who absolutely, radically believe everything He says. Just read the Beatitudes in Matthew 5: Jesus' teachings are insane in the eyes of the world. And yet, through the power of the Holy Spirit, it works. Christians shouldn't be normal.

> "You are the light of the world. A city that is set on a hill cannot be hidden."
> Jesus Christ

"And we have known and believed the love that God has for us. God is love, and he who abides in love abides in God, and God in him," John wrote in 1 John 4:16. Everything in life comes back to that one

call: knowing how much God loves us. He is intentionally bringing each of us into that knowledge. Once we're there, we no longer need to be rescued from anything: we know that God's love and provision will overcome anything we face. He gives us the key to break out of our own prison.

Sometimes, finding that provision takes time: not everything is instantaneous in the Spirit. The longer the situation stretches out, the greater the revelation God is going to give us and the more power we will have to help others break out of those same circumstances. Life in the Spirit is supposed to be magnificent. If it isn't yet, then it is preparation for that magnificence.

Jude 21 offers a piece of very reasonable advice: *"Keep yourselves in the love of God, looking for the mercy of our Lord Jesus Christ unto eternal life."* Every day, the love of God can renew us – if we will retain our sense of wonder over His glory. We can depend on the nature of God. Our lives can be dependent on His love for us. John wrote in 1 John 4:18: *"There is no fear in love; but perfect love casts out fear, because fear involves torment. But he who fears has not been made perfect in love."*

It is imperative that each of us discover how precious we are to God. *"You are a chosen generation, a royal priesthood, a holy nation, His own special people, that you may proclaim the praises of Him who called you out of darkness into His marvelous light; who once were not a people but are now the people of God, who had not obtained mercy but now have obtained mercy,"* Peter says in 1 Peter 2:9–10. We are God's beloved.

the good news

Once we have learned to live in the joy of dependency, it is our duty to share God's love with everyone around us. Our role on earth is to be God's beloved: this is our great call to ministry. We are prophetically called to share the love of Christ with those who do not yet understand it: *"I will call them My people, who were not My people, and her beloved, who was not beloved,"* says Romans 9:25. Jesus Christ is the Beloved, and we are now a part of Him, according to Ephesians 1:6 – *"to the praise of the glory of His grace, by which He made us accepted in the Beloved."* We share our love now because God first loved us.

Our mission on earth is clear and concise. *"Therefore, as the elect of God, holy and beloved, put on tender mercies, kindness, humility, meekness, longsuffering; bearing with one another, and forgiving one another, if anyone has a complaint against another; even as Christ forgave you, so you also must do,"* Paul wrote in Colossians 3:12–13. *"But we are bound to give thanks to God always for you, brethren beloved by the Lord, because God from the beginning chose you for salvation through sanctification by the Spirit and belief in the truth, to which He called you by our gospel, for the obtaining of the glory of our Lord Jesus Christ,"* he added in 2 Thessalonians 2:13–14.

The Bible is full of such commands to live and walk as the Beloved of Christ. Nowhere is this more apparent than in John's first epistle. *"Behold what manner of love the Father has bestowed on us, that we should be called children of God!"* John wrote in 1 John 3:1. We must behold this love in order for it to become a reality in our lives.

> "I thank You, Father, Lord of heaven and earth, that You have hidden these things from the wise and prudent and have revealed them to babes."
> Jesus Christ

To not fully accept this love is to reject it, a sin that grieves the Holy Spirit greatly. We grieve Him when we do not see what God wants to be for us. It's not about performance – He doesn't only provide and care for us when we see His contribution. He is there, even then. But God wants to step into the middle of our failures and show us His plan and love, so that we can live in confidence knowing that His love is so deep it covers everything. We should look in the mirror every morning and know, "I am the beloved of God. I have seen the beloved and it is me. God loves me."

The good news of the gospel is that we are radically loved by God. He is very fond of each of us. When God looks at us through the lens of Christ, He doesn't see a failure or a loser and He certainly doesn't see someone who can't hack it or make it. He sees us as His beloved child.

If we are not in touch with being beloved in Christ, we cannot love others as God desires. He wants us to bestow on others what He has given to us. God wants to say, "Graham, have all of this and give away as much as you like because there is plenty more where that came from." If we are strangers to God's love, we are going to be strangers to others.

We are not here on earth to explain the gospel: God doesn't need to be explained or understood. Instead, we are born again to fully experience the good news of knowing God's love so profoundly that our lives become a proclamation of all the excellencies of God's nature. We are the chosen people of God, reveling in His mercy. Anything less than being the fullest expression of God's love is not descriptive of heaven and diminishes God's glory on earth. *"He who has seen Me has seen the Father,"* Jesus said (John 14:9). *"As He is, so are we in this world,"* said John in 1 John 4:17.

> "For God so loved the world that He gave His only begotten Son, that whoever believes in Him should not perish but have everlasting life."
> Jesus Christ

"Do all things without complaining and disputing, that you may become blameless and harmless, children of God without fault in the midst of a crooked and perverse generation, among whom you shine as lights in the world, holding fast the word of life, so that I may rejoice in the day of Christ that I have not run in vain or labored in vain," said Paul in Philippians 2:14–16. We must

become lights of God's love, bright with the truth of who He truly is.

We know from Matthew 16:13–20 that there are many distorted images of Christ. When Jesus asked His disciples to tell Him who the people thought He was, four wrong answers were given: *"Some say John the Baptist, some Elijah, and others Jeremiah or one of the prophets."* Unimpressed, Jesus took the disciples a step further. *"But who do you say that I am?"* Peter immediately spoke the truth. *"You are the Christ, the Son of the living God,"* he said.

The image of God that we carry in our heart is what the rest of the world will see and be attracted to. When His love flows from us, we won't have to persuade people to come to church. Our evangelistic efforts have gone askew: we now try to persuade people to come to church. I don't want that; I want people to find Jesus. In the process of finding Him, they can join a family they can be proud of. It shouldn't be our goal to get people into a meeting. Our goal should be to show people something that makes them wonder, something that makes them ask questions, something that makes them pursue God. God's love is unconditional and generous – it goes out, seeking nothing in return.

God's love was so different from anything that had

> "If you knew the gift of God, and who it is who says to you, 'Give Me a drink,' you would have asked Him, and He would have given you living water."
> Jesus Christ

ever been experienced that the New Testament writers had to invent a word for it: *agape*. *Agape* love is "Love as revealed in Jesus, seen as spiritual and selfless and a model for humanity," as the dictionary puts it. *Agape* love leaves our mouths agape: we find ourselves in a state of wonder and amazement over it.

We must not pervert this kind of love with a performance mentality. There is no spiritual truth in the statement, "I've got to do something to get something." We receive from God that which we give; everything comes from Him. In our minds, we have to come before Him and know that when God gives us something, the best way to hold on to it is to give it away. If we try and hoard it, we'll lose it. But if we give it away, it will keep flowing back to us.

Kingdom life is the complete opposite of how the world perceives and acts. In the world, we love people as long as they keep doing things for us. If their contribution diminishes, we pull back. We fall in – and out of – love. Human love expects a return.

Jesus is the complete opposite. *"I will never leave you nor forsake you,"* Jesus said. If we sin, Jesus is there. After all, where sin abounds, grace much more abounds. Jesus is there to love us in the moment we are ready to be loved. He loves without expectation of reward.

We are called to a love that loves people even in their failures. Agape love is mutual – we give, and it is given to us. *"It is more blessed to give than to receive,"* as Acts 20:35 says. In blessing others, we are blessed.

God's intentions toward us never change. Once we realize we are His first love, He can become ours. When we see and know that we are His first love, we become a gift of God to the earth. We become His good news. Power flows from our revelation that we are His beloved, because the beloved has unprecedented favor and unparalleled love.

By accepting God's love with a sense of wonder, we lose our drivenness and performance mentality. We become as the psalmist sang, *"They looked to Him and were radiant, and their faces were not ashamed"* (Psalm 34:5). God is the light of the world, and those who love Him inherit that same radiance.

Performance is necessary if our standard is excellence. Excellence demands effort, training and practice. Our mindset must be right. Without excellence in training, an athlete cannot perform well in competition. In spiritual terms, regarding our relationship with God, it is not our performance that makes us mature, but our acceptance of who we are in Christ. We do not do things to try to get somewhere with God in relationship.

God put us into Christ, on His own initiative. There is no place to get to, we are already there! We must learn how to enjoy abiding. We are in Christ already. We have devotional times because we are in Christ. We serve God because we are in Christ. We pray to demonstrate the relationship we have, not to try to get into one.

Paul writes in Romans 11:36, *"For of Him and through Him and to Him are all things, to whom be glory for ever."* He teaches in Romans 11:35 that we never give to God something that originates with us. We receive something from the Lord; He works it into our lives and pushes it through our hearts. In lifestyle and service what He has released goes back to Him, exactly like the natural process of evaporation, and exactly the process of the thoughts and words of God expressed by Isaiah in 55:8–13. What a great love He has bestowed on us.

> "Behold, I say to you, lift up your eyes and look at the fields, for they are already white for harvest! And he who reaps receives wages, and gathers fruit for eternal life, that both he who sows and he who reaps may rejoice together."
> Jesus Christ

Let's return to a level of simple goodness, recovering a way of being, seeing, speaking, and doing that flows from living the life of a much-loved child. We must be gloriously dependent on the love of the Father. It is God's intention that we be fully encouraged, with our hearts knit together in love.

conclusion

The Kingdom of God belongs to the innocent, to those with a pure heart. This sense of wonder leads us away from the internal darkness of our own carnality and into a deeply dependent relationship with the Holy Spirit.

We are able to discern the truth and speak it in love. We are able to change the world with the goodness of God. We are able to share the fruit of the Spirit with those around us.

Why is it that a lot of us don't do more in the Spirit? I think it's because we're scared that nothing will happen. We think we're only doubting ourselves, but we are actually doubting God's ability to shine through us. Where is our child-like wonder over the power of God?

What is it God is calling you to be through the circumstances of your life? What does He want to finish in you? What do you need God to be for you right now? Whatever issue or worry is facing you at the moment, you can rest assured that God has attached His provision to it. What is knocking at your door? Choose the higher route – choose the provision, not the problem.

Be joyful in your dependence on God. He absolutely adores you. It doesn't matter what you think about yourself – He cannot love you less than 100 per cent. You are not a failure unless you fail to see the love of God for you. He wants so badly for you to see His love for you. Love Him, for He first loved you.

Staying away from sin doesn't make us mature Christians; living out of our confidence in Him does. If we know that everything in our lives flows from God, we can dwell in a spiritual place that removes our sin by clothing us with His righteousness. What if we walked through life cloaked in His peace and joy?

What if we were shielded by His glory? This is the grace of innocence that God wants to return to us. When I spoke with Richard Wurmbrand, I marveled at his peace and serenity – but I also felt unclean sitting with him. What had I gone through for the sake of Christ? What had I accomplished? I felt like I wasn't really saved – I finally understood that I was missing something in my life. Richard inspired me to be a better Christian.

Without a sense of wonder about God, we are blind to His real purposes. We are short-sighted, unable to see beyond the blatantly obvious. What are the things of innocence in us that have been beaten down? How can we set it free?

Life with God is supposed to be simple, Jesus taught. *"Abide in Me, and I in you. As the branch cannot bear fruit of itself, unless it abides in the vine, neither can you, unless you abide in Me,"* He said in John 15:4. God is full of wonder when He looks at His creation – and the whole of creation lives with a similar sense of wonder about God.

> "The soul is healed by being with children."
> Fyodor Dostoevsky

When He formed the world, He sat back and smiled: *"And God saw that it was good,"* Genesis 1 records repeatedly. The Bible is full of references to creation's love for the Father: rocks cry out, nature sings and bows, seas roar, trees clap. The earth knows He's wonderful because He is full of wonder. We can go out into this creation and be gripped by that same wonder for God. His majesty can speak to us through His earth.

After that coffee with Richard Wurmbrand, I made a decision: I no longer wanted to live without a sense of wonder about who God is. At the core of who we are, God wants to restore our DNA of worship, adoration, innocence, and wonder. I want to live astonished and amazed. If that makes me naïve – and even stupid in some people's eyes – so be it. Simplicity and innocence should be the foundation of our relationship with God. He is a happy God and I think He deserves a happy people who dream of what is possible with Him.

> "We live in a wonderful world that is full of beauty, charm and adventure. There is no end to the adventures that we can have if only we seek them with our eyes open."
> Jawaharlal Nehru

We must look for the good in people. To find that treasure, we must be governed by who we want to be in Jesus. Other people's perspectives need to fall by the wayside in the light of who Jesus is to us. Life has taught us to be suspicious, distrustful, wary, cynical, contemptuous, and watchful. But these attitudes of the heart harm us, and we need to renounce them. Let's put on God and be transformed by Him. When we sow contempt, we reap it back on ourselves. If we find it easy to be negative, people will be negative about us.

The time has come for Christians to be revived in a child-like spirituality. Wrap yourself in a sense of wonder about who God is. Dream about Him. Worship

Him. Ask Him for His purity and child-like excitement. Let His grace pervade every aspect of your life. Tell Him how much you love Him. Thank Him for His creation and His gifts and His blessing. Innocence is yours for the taking – you only need to ask Him for it.

Childlike Learning

To become a fully mature son
You must first learn the ways of a child.

Learn to be open, trusting and small.
Feel the joy of smallness wrapped in the immensity of Me.

Learn to exchange your inadequacy for vulnerability
It is weakness with laughter.
Clap your hands and shout at the pleasure of being small
Then lift your arms in confidence and I will bear you up.

Let your eyes be bright
Allow My love to overwhelm
Enjoy the feel of fear dying and confidence increasing
Face the day in total rest.

Grace is good for Me
It enables Me to touch you continuously
To speak, to draw near
To be present always.
To enjoy your child-like heart
To be One with you.

Grace is good for you
It makes you feel good about yourself
You are not what you were, by grace
You are not yet what you will be, that will be by grace
Therefore you are who you are, now ... by grace.
Grace provides you with the confidence to know that
You are always welcome, always wanted.
Enjoy the grace you have and use it boldly
As a favored child.

Learn to see as a child would
To look beyond the natural
Train your eyes to see My hand
Your ears to hear My voice
For I am always working and endlessly speaking.

Hear Me as I speak to others and be My voice to them
For all that you share will gladden your heart
Watch what I am doing around you
Be ready to be included and I will astonish you.

Be prepared to be amazed.
Allow me to use your will to touch your mind
As they deliberately collaborate your emotions will serve your spirit
This is divine order, practice it daily
And wonder will grow.

Laugh more, worry less
Wonder has expectation that releases faith
Practice simplicity and you will never be confused.
Complexity increases procrastination
You will always put off what you don't understand
Simplicity turns faith into works
For it enables you to see the next small step you must take.

Above all ... ENJOY!!
Enjoy being Mine, love your belonging
Enjoy finding peace, always there
Enjoy the grace of the present moment
No matter what is occurring.

When you live in Christ and not your circumstances
Then you can enjoy the moment and see a better outcome
No matter how hard the situation.

The fruit of wonder is joy unspeakable
Joy is the source of strength
Everything is a cycle
All you need comes from Me
It works in you through Me
And returns from you to Me
Being child-like is to make sure
That in that cycle you do not
Disconnect, but remain with Me.

exercise 1: simple ways to strengthen your sense of wonder

A heightened sense of wonder is absolutely vital to a renewed relationship with God. The power of God should constantly fascinate us. Here are some suggestions of ways to further develop your own sense of wonder:

1. Spend a day with a child. See things through their eyes. Take them to a playground or toy store; buy them candy. Watch how they love new things.
2. Connect with nature. Find a park or beach and let the rhythm of God's creation wash over you. Ask Him to walk the trails with you.
3. Learn to be thankful (see Exercise 2 for ideas).
4. Go to a book or music store and try some new products. Listen to music you wouldn't normally listen to. Read excerpts of books on topics you find inspiring. Spend the day there, asking God to show you more of Him through other people's creativity.
5. Enjoy the company of good friends. Remember, where two or three are gathered, Jesus is there.
6. Throw a feast. Celebrate a rite of passage in your life by inviting people to a party. Treat them with the same joy with which God treats you.

7. Find an old castle or cathedral and sit in it for a while. Enjoy the architecture and history.

8. Do what you love. If you love to golf, go golfing. If you love to paint, buy a new canvas. If you love to write, start scribbling. Meditate on the greatness of God.

9. Secretly bless someone. Pay attention to the needs and desires of those close to you. Become a kind-of secret admirer, filling that want. Enjoy their reaction.

10. Visit your church. Sit on the edge of the stage and look around the empty room. Breathe it in. Thank God for the blessings He's poured out. Envision it with your friends in it – and speak blessing over them.

exercise 2: practicing the art of thanksgiving

Developing an attitude of gratitude goes a long way toward restoring a sense of wonder in our lives. Being thankful sheds light on our lives, illuminating places where God has been quietly working to bless us. Here are some easy exercises to help us become more thankful:

1. Write a list of ten family members, friends, neighbors, or church-goers and write one thing about each that inspires you to be more Christ-like. Look at them with the same kind of wonder that Jesus looks at them with.
2. Pick up a box of thank you cards and start writing, thanking people for the intangible gifts from God they are to you. Try to send a box of cards out every three months.
3. Start a gratitude journal, writing one thing you're thankful for every day for a year. This will be easy to do on good days, and inspiring to read on bad ones.
4. Write a letter of thanks to someone (teacher, friend, parent, youth pastor, Sunday School worker) who greatly influenced you as a child. Track down their address and send it to them.

5. When sorting through e-mail every day, take a moment and write a thankful note to someone.

6. Write a letter to your children or grandchildren, thanking them for something they have recently shown you. Tell them things you love about them. If your children are very young, keep the letter and give it to them when they're older.

7. Put an appreciative note in your spouse's coat, briefcase, or lunch bag. Tell them how much they mean to you.

8. Begin your prayer time by listing things you are thankful for. The Psalms say that "We enter His gates with thanksgiving," so take note of how close God feels as you thank Him for the blessings in your life.

9. Help someone in need. Go on a grocery shopping spree and buy some good stuff for the local food bank. Put together a secret hamper for some in-need friends. Be creative.

10. Write a thanksgiving psalm. The ancient Israelite worship leaders would sing prayers of thanks to God; we can do the same today.

FAQ:

frequently asked questions

Q. *Who is Graham Cooke and how can I find more information about him?*

A. Graham is a speaker and author who lives in Vacaville, California. He has been involved in prophetic ministry since 1974. He has developed a series of training programs on prophecy, leadership, spirituality, devotional life, walking in the Spirit, and spiritual warfare. All of which have received international acclaim for their depth of insight, revelation and wisdom.

    Graham serves on the leadership team of The Mission in Vacaville where he is part of a think tank exploring the future and developing strategies for onward momentum and progression.

    You can learn more about Graham at www.grahamcooke.com.

Q. *How can I become a prayer partner with Graham?*

A. Check his website, www.grahamcooke.com, for all of the information you need.

Q. *Has Graham written any other books?*

A. To date Graham has written 4 books; co-authored 2 more and written 8 Interactive Journals. These are:

Books:

➤ Developing Your Prophetic Gifting (now out of print).

➤ A Divine Confrontation ... Birth Pangs of the New Church.

➤ Approaching the Heart of Prophecy [Volume 1 in the Prophetic Series].

➤ Prophecy & Responsibility [Volume 2 in the Prophetic Series].

Journals:

➤ Hiddenness & Manifestation [Book 1 "Being with God" Series].

➤ Crafted Prayer [Book 2 "Being with God" Series].

➤ The Nature of God [Book 3 "Being with God" Series].

➤ Beholding and Becoming [Book 4 "Being with God" Series].

➤ Towards a Powerful Inner Life [Book 5 "Being with God" Series].

➤ The Language of Promise [Book 6 "Being with God" Series].

➤ Living in Dependency and Wonder [Book 7 "Being with God" Series].

➤ God's Keeping Power [Book 8 "Being with God" Series].

Co-author:

➤ Permission Granted with Gary Goodell

➤ When Heaven Opens with Lucas Sherraden

All are available at www.brilliantbookhouse.com.

about the author

Graham lives in Vacaville, California where he is
part of the leadership team of The Mission, a resource
church that touches the nations. He has responsibility
for some of the training initiatives and is part of a think
tank that explores the future and develops strategies in
the present.

He is a popular conference speaker and is well known
for developing innovative and authentic training
programs on the prophetic, leadership, contemporary
spirituality, devotional life, spiritual warfare, and living
in the Spirit.

He also functions as a consultant, specifically helping
churches make the transition from one dimension of
calling to a higher level of vision and ministry. He has a
passion to build prototype churches that can fully reach
our postmodern world.

A strong part of Graham's ministry is in producing finances and resources to help the poor, supporting many projects around the world. He also financially supports and helps to underwrite church planting, leadership development, evangelism, and health and rescue projects in underdeveloped countries. If you wish to become a financial partner for the sake of missions, please contact Graham's office where his personal assistant, Jeanne Thompson, will be able to assist you.

Graham has many prayer partners who play a significant part in his ministry. For more information, please contact Pam Jarvis, Prayer Coordinator, at prayer@grahamcooke.com.

Contact details for Graham Cooke:

<u>United States:</u>

Future Training Institute

6391 Leisure Town Road

Vacaville, CA 95687

USA

E-mail: office@grahamcooke.com

<u>United Kingdom:</u>

Sword of Fire Ministries

P.O. Box 1

Southampton, SO16 7WJ

E-mail: admin@swordfire.org.uk